BLOOM'S Re Views

COMPREHENSIVE RESEARCH & STUDY GUIDES

Charles Dickens's
A Tale of Two Cities

Edited & with
an Introduction
by Harold Bloom

First Printing
1 3 5 7 9 8 6 4 2

ISBN: 0-7910-4166-2

Chelsea House Publishers
1974 Sproul Road, Suite 400
P.O. Box 914
Broomall, PA 19008-0914

Contents

Editor's Note

My Introduction centers upon Madame Defarge as the incarnation of the French Revolution, in Dickens's vision. Critical extracts begin with early reviews of the novel, and go on to G. K. Chesterton's admiring realization that Dickens had no understanding of the French "reasonable impatience" that led to the Revolution.

Arthur Waugh praises the taut plotting of *A Tale of Two Cities*, after which George Orwell meditates upon Dickens's ambivalence towards the French Revolution. Jack Lindsay traces the literary background of the novel, while Monroe Engel idealistically emphasizes the theme of personal resurrection as being central to the book.

John Gross contrasts the two heroes, Carton and Darnay, and then Earle Davis considers the overwhelming influence of Thomas Carlyle upon Dickens's novel. In Robert Alter's judgment, the portraits of violence are more memorable than anything else in the book.

Sylvère Monod reminds us of how much Dickensian humor and melodrama the novel encompasses, while Edwin Eigner concludes that Darnay is a rather inconclusive Revolutionary hero. In J. M. Rignall's judgment, the book does not reconcile its hopes for social peace and its intense obsession with social violence.

Ruth Glancy concentrates upon the heroine, Lucy Manette, after which we are given a very contrasting portrait, of the fierce Madame Defarge, by Tom Lloyd. Time is seen as the novel's great villain by James Marlow, who concludes these excerpts upon the book's great "counter-theme" of resurrection.

Introduction

Though it is, by any standards, a remarkable performance, *A Tale of Two Cities* at first may seem distinctly *not* a novel by Charles Dickens. Where are the great grotesques, the endless digressions, above all the humor? Dark and unrelenting, the *Tale* is pure storytelling, as economical in its way as is Shakespeare's *Macbeth*. Dickens even provides us with *his* Lady Macbeth in Madame Defarge, the fiercely attractive genius of the French Revolution, as the *Tale* portrays it. Nor are Madame Defarge and her husband, the wineshop keeper Defarge, the villains of the book. For once, Dickens has no villains, or history itself is the villain. Though the story manifests an obsessive dread of revolutionary violence, it also displays a considerable loathing for the social oppression that, in part, provoked the French Revolution and the Reign of Terror. Much under the influence of Thomas Carlyle's visionary chronicle, *The French Revolution,* Dickens's narrative shares in Carlyle's prophetic warning to England that economic tyranny ensues at last in the answering tyranny of the mob. Whether *A Tale of Two Cities* now can be interpreted as an admonition for the United States, as it moves toward the Millennium, is for the individual student or reader to judge.

If the *Tale* has no authentic villains, despite the colorful menace of the Defarges and their followers, it also lacks heroes and a heroine, though such a view would have disheartened Dickens, who certainly intended Lucie Manette as the heroine and Sydney Carton and Charles Darnay, the two men who love her, as heroes. Unfortunately, the three of them together are likely to interest us rather less than Madame Defarge does, because they lack her intensity of being. If we read more closely, then we will find that Carton is profoundly interesting, though neither Lucie nor her husband, Charles Darnay, is redeemed as dramatic characters by a prolonged scrutiny. Carton, despite his celebrated and sentimental prophetic thoughts that close the book, is more than the dark side of his double and successful rival, Darnay. We can surmise that

Carton is the near-nihilist that Dickens senses he himself might become. Whether Carton's self-sacrifice is psychologically persuasive is disputable, but it is dramatically convincing and has become a permanent image of renunciation, as Dickens intended it should be. Though he dies *as* Darnay, and considers himself to be dying *for* Lucie, Carton in a true sense dies so that his creator, Charles Dickens, shall continue to live.

Madame Defarge, everyone's favorite character in the novel, dies a victim of her own consuming passion for revenge. Carton's closing prophecy tells us that Defarge and his group will also die, by the agency of the guillotine they have worshipped and fed. Since Dickens had little more than Carlyle's vision of the French Revolution to sustain him, *A Tale of Two Cities* is not history and hardly asks to be taken as such. The book is a historical romance in its genre, yet it would never have achieved its perpetual popularity if it were entirely composed in that mode. John Ruskin, the great Victorian critic, rightly praised Dickens as being a master of "stage fire," and *A Tale of Two Cities* in its essence is a melodrama, very appropriate for dramatic presentation, whether in the theater or on screen. The actual leaders and contending forces of the French Revolution do not appear in the book, which so arranges matters as to make us believe that a better informed police could have prevented the entire upheaval by one efficient raid upon the Defarge wineshop. That would be absurd history, but the book's identification of the Revolution with the Defarges is as dramatically successful as Shakespeare's concentration upon Macbeth and Lady Macbeth, while blending everyone else in the play into a common grayness. The single image everyone remembers of *A Tale of Two Cities* is Madame Defarge's knitting. She is the malevolent, would-be Fate of the novel, and her knitting hints at the weaving of the Fates, a role occupied by the witches in *Macbeth*. It is not too much to say that Madame Defarge is not only the aesthetic glory of Dickens's *Tale,* but in a clear way is the symbol or emblem that unifies the entire book. She is the image of death itself: remorseless, both frightening and yet masochistically attractive, and finally to be conquered only by heroic love, embodied (in the Dickens manner) by the very English Miss Pross, as indomitable as

Winston Churchill or as Dickens himself. The vision of renunciation and resurrection that Dickens sought to convey in Sydney Carton is far better served by Miss Pross, who is willing to die for the Darnay family but instead lives for them, and by her triumph allows them to live. ✤

Biography of
Charles Dickens

Charles John Huffam Dickens was born in Landport, Portsea, near Portsmouth, England, on February 7, 1812, the second of eight children of John and Elizabeth Barrow Dickens. The family moved to London in 1814, to Chatham in 1817, and then back to London in 1822. By 1824 increasing financial difficulties caused Dickens's father to be briefly imprisoned for debt; Dickens himself was put to work for a few months at a shoe-blacking warehouse. Memories of this painful period in his life were to influence much of his later writing, in particular the early chapters of *David Copperfield.*

After studying at the Wellington House Academy in London (1824–27), Dickens worked as a solicitor's clerk (1827–28), then worked for various newspapers, first the *True Sun* (1832–34) and later, as a political reporter, for the *Morning Chronicle* (1834–36). In 1833 Dickens fell in love with Maria Beadnell, but her family opposed any contemplated marriage. Dickens never forgot Maria, and she served as the model for Dora in *David Copperfield.*

In 1836 a collection of articles contributed to various periodicals appeared in two volumes as *Sketches by "Boz," Illustrative of Every-day Life and Every-day People.* This was followed by the enormously popular *Posthumous Papers of the Pickwick Club* (1836–37). Like many of Dickens's later novels, the *Pickwick Papers* first appeared in a series of monthly chapbooks or "parts." Other novels were serialized in magazines before appearing in book form. In 1836 Dickens married Catherine Hogarth, with whom he had ten children before their separation in 1858. At the beginning of his marriage, Catherine's sixteen-year-old sister Mary lived with them, but she died after a few months. The shock of this loss affected Dickens permanently, and Mary would be the model for many of the pure, saintly heroines in his novels—such as Little Nell in *The Old Curiosity Shop*—who die at an early age.

Between 1837 and 1839 Dickens published a second novel, *Oliver Twist,* in monthly installments in *Bentley's Miscellany,* a new periodical of which he was the first editor. This was followed in 1838–39 by *Nicholas Nickleby.* Dickens then founded his own weekly, *Master Humphrey's Clock* (1840–41), in which appeared his novels *The Old Curiosity Shop* and *Barnaby Rudge.* In 1842 he and his wife visited the United States and Canada, and after returning Dickens published *American Notes* (1842), two volumes of impressions that caused much offense in the United States. He then wrote *Martin Chuzzlewit* (1843–44), a novel set partly in America.

In 1843 Dickens published *A Christmas Carol,* the first in a series of Christmas books that included *The Chimes* (1845), *The Cricket on the Hearth* (1846), *The Battle of Life* (1846), and *The Haunted Man and the Ghost's Bargain* (1848). Early in 1846 he was for a brief time the editor of the *Daily News,* a paper of the Radical party to which he contributed "Pictures of Italy" after visiting Italy in 1844 and again in 1845. During a visit to Switzerland in 1846 Dickens wrote his novel *Dombey and Son,* which appeared monthly between 1846 and 1848. In 1850 he started the periodical *Household Words;* in 1859 it was incorporated into *All the Year Round,* which Dickens continued to edit until his death. Much of his later work was published in these two periodicals, including *David Copperfield* (1849–50), *Bleak House* (1852–53), *Hard Times* (1854), *Little Dorrit* (1855–57), *A Tale of Two Cities* (1859), *Great Expectations* (1860–61), and *Our Mutual Friend* (1864–65).

Throughout his life, Dickens threw himself vigorously into a variety of social and political crusades, such as prison reform, improvement of education, the status of workhouses, and reform of the copyright law (American publishers were notorious for pirating his works and offering him no compensation). These interests find their way also into his work, which is characterized by sympathy for the oppressed and a keen examination of class distinctions. His novels and stories have been both praised and censured for their sentimentality and their depiction of "larger-than-life" characters, such as Pickwick or Mr. Micawber (in *David Copperfield*).

During the last twenty years of his life Dickens still found time to direct amateur theatrical productions, sometimes of his own plays. He also became involved in a variety of philanthropical activities, gave public readings, and in 1867–68 visited America for a second time. Dickens died suddenly on June 9, 1870, leaving unfinished his last novel, *The Mystery of Edwin Drood,* which was first published later that same year. Several editions of his collected letters have been published. Despite his tremendous popularity during and after his own life, it was not until the twentieth century that serious critical study of his work began to appear. Modern critical opinion has tended to favor the later, more somber and complex works over the earlier ones characterized by boisterous humor and broad caricature. ❖

Thematic and Structural Analysis

The famous first sentence of Charles Dickens's *A Tale of Two Cities* establishes important thematic and structural patterns of the novel:

> It was the best of times, it was the worst of times, it was the age of wisdom, it was the age of foolishness, it was the epoch of belief, it was the epoch of incredulity, it was the season of Light, it was the season of Darkness, it was the spring of hope, it was the winter of despair, we had everything before us, we had nothing before us, we were all going direct to Heaven, we were all going direct the other way. . . .

Just as these phrases achieve their stirring rhetorical effect by broad conceptual oppositions, the novel as a whole achieves its vivid imaginative effects by means of starkly contrasting settings, personalities, and motivations: staid England and turbulent France; hopeful Charles Darnay and self-destructive Sydney Carton; tender Lucie Manette and bloodthirsty Madame Defarge. Even the resurrection and rejuvenation of Dr. Manette and Charles Darnay are contrasted with the destruction of countless innocent people by the cruelties first of France's Old Regime and then of the Republican terror. Dickens uses these contrasts to explore, in the context of revolutionary France, the subject that forms the center of his interest throughout his many novels: the effect large forces such as class, technology, and historical change have on human feeling and action.

Book one, chapter one of *A Tale of Two Cities* evokes the uneasy mood that prevailed in England and France in 1775. Dickens describes it as a time of lawlessness and tyranny, brooding rebellion and apocalyptic prophecies. This mood is sustained in **chapter two** (and throughout the novel) as the narrative moves from the historical to the personal. We are introduced to Mr. Jarvis Lorry, a passenger on the Dover mail coach, who finds himself walking beside the coach as it toils up a muddy incline. It is late at night, and a sense of danger among the company grows sharper as a rider on horseback emerges from the darkness. A messenger approaches the coach and requests the attention of Mr. Lorry, who asks if it is "Jerry" who wants him. The messenger says that it is and that he has a dispatch from "T. and Co." Mr. Lorry assures the coachman that he knows the messenger and that it is safe to let him approach. Again reassuring the coachman and his uneasy fellow passengers that he is associated with Tellson's Bank, a highly reputable firm, and that he is going to Paris on business, Mr. Lorry reads the message: "Wait at Dover for Mam'selle." His reply is brief and enigmatic: "Jerry, say that my answer was, 'RECALLED TO LIFE.' " Mr. Lorry gets back into the coach, where he dozes (**chapter three**), dreaming that there has been a run on the bank and that he is digging someone out of a grave. "I hope you care to live?" he repeatedly asks the man he has rescued in his dream. "I can't say," the man replies.

Chapter four begins as Mr. Lorry—described as an elderly but still energetic and punctilious man—is deposited by the coach at the Royal George Hotel in Dover, where he is treated familiarly but with great respect. He asks that a room be prepared for a lady who will arrive that afternoon. When she comes, he goes immediately to see her—an attractive young woman with blond hair and blue eyes—and his manner toward her is cool and detached, thoroughly businesslike. He begins to tell a story, which the young woman, Lucie Manette, who remembers being brought to England by Mr. Lorry as a young child, almost immediately recognizes as that of her family.

Mr. Lorry tells Lucie about the Doctor of Beauvais, a Frenchman with an account at Tellson's, who suddenly vanished almost twenty years ago. The doctor seemed to have fallen prey to a powerful enemy who had the "privilege of filling up blank forms for the consignment of any one to the oblivion of a prison for any length of time." Even though the doctor's wife, an Englishwoman, searched for her husband until her death two years later, she raised their infant daughter to believe that her father was dead, hoping to spare her pain. He then tells the much shaken Lucie that Tellson's has found her father, who is under the care of a former servant in Paris. He says, "We are going there: I, to identify him if I can: you, to restore him to life, love, duty, rest, comfort."

The scene now shifts to the exterior of a wineshop in the St. Antoine district of Paris with a richly symbolic description of red wine flowing from a broken cask between the cobblestones of the street (**chapter five**). The poor people who live in the area use their hands to scoop the wine into their mouths. On a literal level, the image reflects the extreme degradation in which the common people of France live. On another level, the spilled wine foreshadows the human blood that will flow during the French Revolution. And on yet another level, the people's hands and garments are said to be "stained" by the wine—a term that suggests that the people are tainted or made guilty by their actions in the Revolution.

But the wine also has a more positive religious connotation: the Christian ritual of resurrection and rebirth. In the Christian Mass, the transformation of ordinary wine into the blood of Jesus Christ commemorates his sacrifice for humankind. The wine thus has a double significance: It represents both Christ's suffering and his capacity to redeem humanity. Dickens weaves the Christian symbolism of resurrection throughout the novel, as in Mr. Lorry's odd message: "Recalled to Life." The novel may thus attempt a Christian interpretation of the French Revolution: Just as Christ's suffering was the necessary first step toward redemption, so the suffering of the French people before and during the Revolution marks the beginning of the purification and renewal of European civilization.

Dickens shifts his focus to the wineshop's interior and trains our eyes on its proprietors, Monsieur and Madame Defarge. M. Defarge is a sturdy, vigorous dark-haired man "of strong resolution and a set purpose." His wife, a stout woman wrapped in fur, has an air suggesting that "she did not often make mistakes." Also in the shop are Mr. Lorry and Lucie, who observe a cryptic exchange between M. Defarge and several customers, who all address each other as Jacques. Presently Mr. Lorry approaches the wine merchant, who leads the pair up a staircase to a locked door. Behind it they find a crazed white-haired man sitting on a low bench and busily making shoes. At first he ignores them and continues his work, but when they ask his name, he answers in a "forlorn" voice that he is "One Hundred and Five, North Tower" (**chapter six**). He explains that he was not originally a shoemaker but taught himself the trade upon arriving and has "made shoes ever since." Mr. Lorry addresses him by his former name, "Monsieur Manette," but fails to elicit any remembrance. Only upon beholding his daughter does the prisoner begin to show any signs of recognition. He is still disoriented and distracted as they lead him down the stairs and into a coach, even requesting his shoemaking tools before they drive away. Book one ends with Mr. Lorry asking him the portentous question, "I hope you care to be recalled to life?" His answer is uncertain: "I can't say."

Book two, "The Golden Thread," takes up the story five years later. After a humorous description of Tellson's Bank—"the triumphant perfection of inconvenience"—and of the domestic situation of its "odd-job-man," Jerry Cruncher (**chapter one**), we follow Jerry as he brings a note to Mr. Lorry, who is at the trial of Charles Darnay, a young French gentleman accused of betraying British secrets to the French king (**chapter two**). The government's attorney argues that the accused made multiple trips between Britain and France, pointing to the testimony of two "virtuous" witnesses, John Barsad and Roger Cly (**chapter three**). Dr. and Lucie Manette are also called to testify that Darnay traveled by ship with them when they returned from France five years before. On the stand Lucie recalls the tenderness with which the accused treated her ailing father but also admits that Darnay did confer with two Frenchmen before the ship departed and that he jokingly suggested that one day George Washington would be as famous as George III. When the prosecution calls Barsad and Cly, Mr. Stryver, Darnay's attorney, tries to discredit them by asserting that Barsad is a "hired" spy and Cly his partner. The situation, however, continues to look grim for Darnay until Mr. Sydney Carton, Stryver's slovenly and distracted assistant, cleverly casts doubt on the testimony of another of the prosecution's key witnesses, who claims he saw Darnay in the coffee room of a hotel in a dockyard town five years ago, waiting for a fellow conspirator. Carton casts doubt on this claim by pointing out his own remarkable resemblance to Darnay, forcing the witness to admit that it could just as easily have been Carton whom he saw. The prosecution's case is thrown into question, and Stryver successfully presses the advantage to win Darnay's acquittal.

Dr. Manette, Lucie, Stryver, and Carton gather to congratulate Darnay after the trial (**chapter four**). We learn that in the five years since his departure from France, Lucie's tender care has restored Dr. Manette to his former self and that Darnay has become a close friend of the family. Later that evening as he dines with Carton, Darnay toasts Lucie, but the legal assistant throws his glass over his shoulder. Carton tells Darnay, "I am a disappointed drudge, sir. I care for no man on earth, and no man on earth cares for me." He then tells Darnay that he does not like him, and Darnay departs abruptly. The morose Carton drinks alone and confronts himself in the mirror, admitting his jealousy and resentment of Darnay.

In **chapter five** Dickens describes the relationship between Carton and Stryver, his employer, in which Carton plays "jackal" to Stryver's "lion." Carton, even though he is as intelligent as his employer, lacks the ambition that drives Stryver, who is an up-and-coming lawyer. The absence of this trait, together with his moodiness and dissipated habits, prevents Carton from achieving professional success. Describing Carton dragging himself home at daybreak after a night spent drinking with Stryver, Dickens evokes the pathos of his situation:

> Sadly, sadly, the sun rose; it rose upon no sadder sight than the man of good abilities and good emotions, incapable of their directed exercise, incapable of his own help and his own happiness, sensible of the blight on him, and resigning himself to let it eat him away.

In **chapter six** Mr. Lorry, having become friends with the Manettes, visits them in their home in a quiet corner of Soho. He converses briefly with Lucie's maid, the ferociously loyal and protective Miss Pross. She tells Mr. Lorry that the only man worthy of marrying Lucie is her brother, Solomon, who unfortunately has been damned by a "mistake in life." Dickens informs us that Miss Pross's high estimation of her brother is a charming but misplaced testament to her loyalty: Her brother is actually a heartless scoundrel who absconded with all of her money.

Darnay soon arrives and, as the Manettes and their guests sit in the garden, tells a remarkable story about some workmen who found an old dungeon in the Tower of London where a prisoner, before going to execution, had carved the word *DIG* on the cornerstone. Upon examining the earth underneath the stone, they found the ashes of a paper, mingled with the ashes of a small leather case or bag. The paper, Darnay concludes, must have contained some vital information that the prisoner wished to hide from his jailers. After hearing the story, Dr. Manette becomes extremely agitated and insists that they all go inside. The group heeds his wish, and nothing more is said about the story.

The novel then shifts back to France and focuses upon the decadent and despicable Marquis de St. Evrémonde, a French nobleman who is also called Monseigneur (**chapters seven to nine**). We first see him being fed hot chocolate by four different servants and taking the most excruciating care with his clothing and appearance. The marquis leaves his magnificent residence in Paris and drives through the city to the countryside. On the way, the marquis is forced to stop when his coach runs over and kills a child. As the child's father bends howling over the dead body, the marquis throws a gold coin toward the gathered group of peasants and castigates them for not taking better care of their children. M. Defarge is on the scene and attempts to console the father by telling him the child is actually better off. The marquis compliments Defarge on this philosophical outlook, tosses another gold coin, and sets off again in the carriage. As the coin flies back through the window, however, the nobleman stops again and looks out of his coach at the spot where M. Defarge had been standing. He sees instead the father weeping and a dark, stout woman— Mme. Defarge—grimly knitting. "You dogs!" he shouts, "I would ride over any of you very willingly, and exterminate you from the earth."

As the marquis advances through the desolate countryside, he passes through an impoverished village and notices one of the peasants staring fixedly at his carriage. He stops and questions the man, who tells him that he saw a tall, pale man hanging by a chain under the carriage—"white as a spectre, tall as a spectre!"—who escaped over the hillside as soon as the carriage stopped. The marquis continues on his way, ignoring the supplications of a starving peasant woman at a rustic graveyard, until he arrives at an imposing stone chateau.

As the door opens, he asks if "Monsieur Charles" has arrived from England. When Monsieur Charles, known in England by the pseudonym Charles Darnay, does arrive, he immediately enters into a heated argument with the marquis, who is his uncle (**chapter nine**). Because of his family's cruel and oppressive behavior, Darnay has decided to renounce his name and inheritance, which he dubs "a crumbling tower of waste, mismanagement, extortion, mortgage, oppression, nakedness, and suffering." He plans to stay in England where he will work for his living and warns that "there is a curse" on the ancestral lands and perhaps on all of France. The marquis scoffs at his nephew, but Darnay's intimation of a "curse" is borne out the next morning, when the marquis is found with a knife in his heart. The note attached to the hilt of the knife suggests that he has been murdered in revenge for the driving accident: *Drive him fast to his tomb. This, from* JACQUES."

From here until the end of book two, the narrative splits into two strands; one takes place in England, the other in France. Much of the action in England revolves around the courtship and marriage of Lucie. Darnay, who has established himself in England as a successful teacher of French language and literature, makes the first move (**chapter ten**). He is in love with Lucie but has not yet told her so. One summer day he plucks up the courage to approach Lucie's father. But Dr. Manette is hesitant, so Darnay requests only that if Lucie asks about him, she should be told of his desire to marry her. Dr. Manette agrees on the condition that if they do marry, Darnay will not tell him his real last name until the morning of their wedding.

While these promises are being made, Stryver announces to Carton that he intends to marry Lucie (**chapter eleven**). Stryver's high hopes are soon deflated, however, when he stops by Mr. Lorry's office to tell him his plans (**chapter twelve**). Mr. Lorry gently conveys his doubts that Lucie will accept his proposal and persuades Stryver to wait until he can confirm his hunch. He finds that his doubts are correct and reports this information to Stryver that night. Glad to have avoided embarrassment, Stryver gives up his plan.

Carton now takes the opportunity to make his own feelings known (**chapter thirteen**). In a characteristically sorrowful, awkward, and self-reproachful fashion, he professes his undying love to Lucie, although he does not even pretend to propose formally, knowing that he has no great prospects and cannot change his dissolute way of life. Lucie is nonetheless touched by the sincerity of his words and promises always to think of him kindly.

Some time later, Lucie and Darnay are married. The night before (**chapter seventeen**), Lucie sits with her father, sharing a moment of perfect peace and happiness. The next day (**chapter eighteen**), however, as soon as the wedding is over and Lucie and Darnay have departed, Dr. Manette lapses into a fit of shoemaking. Mr. Lorry keeps his condition secret from Lucie, but he cannot bring the doctor out of his delusion. Ten days later, however, the doctor is restored to his usual self. Mr. Lorry indirectly asks the doctor whether he should be concerned about further relapses, but the doctor assures him that the problem is unlikely to arise again (**chapter nineteen**).

Darnay and Lucie soon return and settle into a peaceful contentment (**chapters twenty and twenty-one**). Carton asks Darnay's forgiveness for his drunken rudeness after the trial. When Darnay later describes the incident, Lucie asks him to think more kindly of Carton, certain that "he is capable of good things, gentle things, even magnanimous things." As the years pass, the Darnays have a daughter and a son. After a time the boy dies, but the girl thrives.

Interspersed with the story of the Darnays' marriage is the narrative's second strand: a description of the rising rage and resentment in France. In **chapter fifteen** (soon after Carton's declaration of love) we return to the wineshop in Paris, where Mme. Defarge sits, like a Greek Fate, tirelessly knitting. She is knitting a coded history—a chronicle of the events that are leading to the country's upheaval and a list of those who have committed crimes against France's people. Through Mme.

Defarge, Dickens suggests that no action or event is historically indifferent or inconsequential, but is instead part of a larger pattern.

A country road builder tells a story that provides a new stitch in France's fate: After nearly a year of hiding and in spite of petitions presented to the king and queen, the enraged father who vengefully killed the marquis was apprehended and hanged. The Defarges and some of their assembled associates discuss how this event should be recorded in Mme. Defarge's record and agree that the chateau and the Evrémond family should be registered as "doomed to destruction." M. Defarge is especially impatient for revenge (**chapter sixteen**), but Mme. Defarge urges him to be patient. As the voice of historical fate, she knows that vengeance is inevitable, but will only occur at the proper time: "[A]lthough it is a long time on the road, it is on the road and coming. I tell thee it never retreats, and never stops."

A man named Barsad, whom the Defarges have been warned is a spy, then enters the wineshop. He tries to engage the couple in an incriminating conversation, but the Defarges do not take the bait. Barsad tells them that he has had news that Lucie Manette is to marry Charles Darnay. When M. Defarge learns Darnay's family identity, he says grimly, ". . . I hope for her [Lucie's] sake, destiny will keep her husband out of France."

In **chapter twenty-one** the two narrative strands begin to come together. The first half of the chapter focuses on the Darnays, while the second half describes the storming of the Bastille, which begins the French Revolution. M. Defarge is at the head of the mob storming the prison and goes directly to Dr. Manette's old cell, which he tears apart in a frantic search for an unidentified object. Then, with M. Defarge leading, the mob embarks on a spree of violence.

The uneasy quiet that settles over the St. Antoine district after this event is soon shattered when M. Defarge tells the people that Foulon, the notorious aristocrat who had said that the people could eat grass, has been captured (**chapter twenty-two**). The men and women of the district take to the streets and proceed to the Hôtel de Ville, where Foulon is being held, drag him outside, stuff his mouth with grass, hang, and behead him. They also seize his hated son-in-law, whom they hang and behead as well. Afterward, the people of the district St. Antoine share what little food they have and exult in their victory. Meanwhile, in the provinces the road builder has joined with other peasants to burn down the chateau of the Marquis de St. Evrémonde (**chapter twenty-three**).

The Revolution roars wildly in France for three years, while in London "[t]hree more birthdays of little Lucie [Lucie and Charles's daughter] are woven by the golden thread into the peaceful tissue of the life of her home" (**chapter twenty-four**). However, this peace is soon disrupted when Mr. Lorry decides he must go to Paris to recover some of Tellson's important documents. He departs, taking Jerry Cruncher, the bank's odd-jobs man, with him. When Darnay learns that a longtime servant of his family has been imprisoned by the rebels, he follows Mr. Lorry, sending word to Lucie and Dr. Manette that he will write them when he arrives (**chapter twenty-five**).

Book three begins with the capture of Darnay on his way to Paris (**chapter one**). Cursed as an emigrant and an aristocrat, he is jailed with a crowd of unusually well mannered prisoners, whom he sees as ghosts of their former aristocratic selves: "The ghost of beauty, the ghost of stateliness, the ghost of elegance, the ghost of pride, the ghost of frivolity, the ghost of wit, the ghost of youth, the ghost of age, all waiting their dismissal from the desolate shore. . . ."

A short time later, Mr. Lorry, installed in Tellson's Paris offices, hears the sounds of the city's unrest and thanks God that no one close to him is in the city. Suddenly Dr. Manette and Lucie burst into the room and inform him that Darnay has been imprisoned. Dr. Manette explains that he has come to use his status as a former prisoner to help Charles. The doctor and Mr. Lorry look out to the courtyard where they see an alarming spectacle—the mounting of an enormous grindstone, to which angry local people are bringing axes, hatchets, knives, bayonets, and swords for sharpening. Mr. Lorry grimly notes that the mob is "murdering the prisoners" and urges the doctor not to lose a minute. The kind-hearted businessman is impressed as he watches Dr. Manette stride into the center of the crowd, declare himself a former prisoner, and rally the volatile people around the idea of freeing his son-in-law.

Lucie, her daughter, and Jerry Cruncher spend this time in a secluded apartment. They are visited by M. and Mme. Defarge, who, aside from delivering a note from Charles assuring his wife and friends that he is well, are unwilling to help; indeed, their manner is cold and mechanical (**chapter three**).

Over the next year and several months (**chapter four**) Dr. Manette prevents Charles from being beheaded and aids the wounded and sick from both sides, thus regaining his former confidence and authority. But all Lucie can do is stand for an hour every day at a particular spot where Charles can see her from his cell. While there she often speaks with a curious "wood sawyer" (the former road-builder) who lives on this street (**chapter five**). He is not a source of great comfort, however, as he has dubbed his saw "Little Guillotine" and laughs as "she" lops off the heads of logs.

Finally Darnay is called before the tribunal (**chapter six**). At first the crowd clamors for his aristocratic blood, but he quickly wins it over by explaining why he left France and stayed in England. Dr. Manette's own testimony completes the defense, and the people bear the liberated Darnay home on their shoulders. But no sooner is Darnay in Lucie's apartment, than a group of four red-capped revolutionaries arrive to take him away, saying that the Defarges and an unnamed "other" have denounced him again and that he will be tried the following day (**chapter seven**).

Meanwhile Miss Pross, unconscious of this turn of events, is bustling through the city. Entering a wineshop, she sees her long-lost brother, Solomon, screams, and attempts to embrace him. He quiets her abruptly, leading her outside where he explains that he is "an official" and that the disclosure of his true identity could get him killed. Jerry Cruncher appears at this moment and becomes deeply suspicious, for he believes he recognizes the man. He insists that Solomon reveal his real name, but before he can respond, Carton, who has just arrived in Paris, appears and says that Solomon's name is Barsad, the spy for the English government who testified against Darnay at his trial. However, Carton asserts that after following Barsad through Paris, he has realized that Barsad is now working for the people's government in France. Threatening to reveal his double-dealing, Carton now forces Solomon/Barsad to assist him in obtaining the release of Darnay.

It remains unclear exactly how Carton intends to free Darnay until the following day. He tells Mr. Lorry and Lucie only that he has arranged with Solomon/Barsad that if Darnay is found guilty, Carton is guaranteed one visit to the prisoner (**chapter nine**). That evening, as Carton prowls the streets of Paris alone, the religious words read at his father's grave run repeatedly through his head: "I am the resurrection and the life: saith the Lord: he that believeth in me, though he were dead, yet shall he live, and whosoever liveth and believeth in me, shall never die."

The next day Carton goes to Darnay's trial, where, to everyone's shock, Dr. Manette is named as a denouncer. Dr. Manette immediately protests, but M. Defarge silences him by telling the tribunal that when he took Dr. Manette out of prison years ago, he examined the cell closely and found a hole in the chimney, in which a document was hidden. He reads the paper, which tells of the abominable cruelty of the Marquis de St. Evrémonde and his brother—their abduction and abuse of a peasant girl and the ensuing deaths of her and her brother (**chapter ten**). The document was written by Dr. Manette himself during his long imprisonment; he had attended the unfortunate girl and was subsequently jailed by the brothers to cover up their crime. It concludes by denouncing the St. Evrémonde brothers and all their descendants, among whom is Darnay. The people clamor for Darnay's blood, and he is sentenced to be executed the following day.

After the trial, Darnay's friends and family are despondent and send Dr. Manette to try once more to persuade the president to reverse the tribunal's decision (**chapter eleven**). Their hopes are only further dashed when they learn that it was Mme. Defarge's brother and sister described in Dr. Manette's letter and that she wants to extend retribution to Darnay's friends and supporters (**chapter twelve**). Dr. Manette's efforts to persuade the president fail, and to everyone's dismay he assumes his old abstracted and compulsive air, requesting his cobbling tools. Only Carton seems able to think about the future and persuades Mr. Lorry to take Lucie, her daughter, and the doctor out of the country with him the following afternoon. Lucie must be convinced that her father's health depends on their leaving. Carton tells Mr. Lorry to have everything ready so that the moment Carton arrives, he can jump into the carriage, and the five can drive away.

In prison Darnay awaits the next day, certain of his death (**chapter thirteen**). He writes a letter to Lucie, professing his undying love and saying that he did not know about her father's imprisonment at the hands of his own relatives. After writing to the doctor and Mr. Lorry, Darnay puts down his pen, believing he is "done with this world."

The next day, however, Darnay hears an English voice as the door to his cell opens, and Carton stands before him. Carton commands Darnay to exchange clothes with him and, once Darnay has, knocks him unconscious and calls in Solomon/Barsad. The spy drags Darnay out of the cell, and shortly thereafter Darnay, disguised as Carton, is placed in Mr. Lorry's carriage and carried swiftly out of Paris, with Lucie, her daughter, Dr. Manette, and Mr. Lorry. Carton, disguised as Darnay, awaits the guillotine.

Meanwhile, the relentless Mme. Defarge has decided to pursue Lucie on her own and sets out for Lucie's flat with a gun and a knife (**chapter fourteen**). There she is confronted by the formidable Miss Pross, who struggles with her and kills her with her own gun.

The next day, Carton exchanges kind and loving words with a peasant seamstress girl and goes calmly to his execution (**chapter fifteen**). Dickens writes that Carton's face as he went to the axe was "the peacefullest man's face ever beheld there. Many added that he looked sublime and prophetic." Indeed, of France itself he prophecies that "a beautiful city and a brilliant people [shall rise] from this abyss."

Carton's famous final words capture the spiritual and emotional redemption he achieves through his self-sacrifice: "It is a far, far better thing that I do, than I have ever done; it is a far, far better rest that I go to than I have ever known." His action and his words recall the imagery of resurrection and renewal that recur throughout the novel. In accordance with the Christian economy of sacrifice, Carton must lose his life in order to find it. Similarly, France must tear itself down in order to rise again. ✤

—*Neal Dolan*
Harvard University

List of Characters

Charles Darnay is a descendant of the French noble family of St. Evrémonde. Horrified by his family's history of cruelty and repression, he moves to England, changes his name, establishes himself as a teacher of French language and literature, and marries Lucie Manette. He is drawn back to revolutionary France by the appeal of a former servant. There he is captured and sentenced to death as an aristocrat and emigrant by the revolutionary mob. Only the self-sacrifice of a rival suitor of Lucie saves him from the guillotine.

Sydney Carton is a bright but moody and dissipated legal assistant to a successful London lawyer, Mr. Stryver. Unable to win the heart of the woman he loves (Lucie Manette), he leads a life of slovenly despair. He redeems himself finally by giving up his own life so that Lucie's husband, Charles Darnay, might live.

Lucie Manette is the sweet-tempered daughter of Dr. Manette, who was imprisoned in the Bastille for twenty years. When he is rescued, she nurses him back to psychological health. She marries Charles Darnay, with whom she has two children, one of whom dies. It is through love for her that Sydney Carton sacrifices his life to save Charles Darnay.

Dr. Manette is a decent and competent French doctor who is imprisoned in the Bastille for twenty years by the Old Regime. While in prison he learns the craft of shoemaking and writes a detailed account of the cruelties he saw performed by the members of the aristocratic St. Evrémonde family. This account is later used to denounce his own innocent son-in-law, Charles Darnay.

Jarvis Lorry is a fastidious, diplomatic, and well-respected businessman and bachelor. He works for Tellson's, the London bank that handles the accounts of many members of the French aristocracy. He takes Dr. Manette's daughter out of France after her father is imprisoned, later returning to rescue him as well. He remains a close friend of the Manette family and is instrumental in the final rescue of Charles Darnay.

Madame Defarge is the novel's symbol of fate. With her husband she leads the revolutionary movement in Paris from their wineshop. Implacable and relentless, she is consumed by the desire for revenge against the aristocratic regime that tortured and killed members of her family. She compulsively knits a chronicle of the significant events of the Revolution.

Monsieur Defarge is the husband of Madame Defarge, co-owner of the wineshop, and co-leader of the revolutionary movement in Paris. He is equally unforgiving and even more impatient for revenge than his wife.

The Marquis de St. Evrémonde (Monseigneur), the uncle of Charles Darnay, embodies the vices of the French aristocracy in the eighteenth century. Cruel, selfish, and arrogant, he treats the common people of France like animals. He is assassinated by the father of a peasant child whom he carelessly rode over in his carriage.

Miss Pross is the sturdy and loyal maid of Lucie Manette. She believes that no one is good enough to marry Lucie except her long-lost brother, Solomon, who turns out to be a spy. She kills the fearful Mme. Defarge at the end of the novel.

Solomon Pross/John Barsad is the ne'er-do-well brother of Miss Pross. Her high regard for him notwithstanding, he takes her money, disappears, and reappears years later, first as a spy for the English government, then as a spy for the revolutionary government in France. Carton sees through his double cross and blackmails him into helping rescue Charles Darnay.

Jerry Cruncher is the rough-hewn messenger and handyman for Tellson's. He moonlights as a "resurrection man"—digging up dead bodies for pay. ✤

Critical Views

[John Forster (1812–1876) was a distinguished British critic and biographer who wrote biographies of Oliver Goldsmith (1848), Walter Savage Landor (1869), and the landmark *Life of Charles Dickens* (1872–74). In this review of *A Tale of Two Cities,* Forster, who has clearly followed Dickens's literary career from its inception, sees the novel as representing the full flower of his literary genius.]

This novel is remarkable for the rare skill with which all the powers of the author's genius are employed upon the conduct of the story. In this respect it is unequalled by any other work from the same hand, and is not excelled by any English work of fiction. The subtlety with which a private history is associated with a most vivid expression of the spirit of the days of the great French Revolution is but a part of its strength in this respect. If the whole purpose of the author had been to show how the tempest of those days of terror gathered and broke, he could not have filled our hearts more truly than he has done with a sense of its wild pitiless fury. But in his broadest colouring of revolutionary scenes, while he gives life to large truths in the story of a nation, he is working out closely and thoroughly the skilfully designed tale of a household. The story is all in all, yet there is nothing sacrificed to it. It is as truly the *Tale of Two Cities* as it is the touching history of Doctor Manette and Lucie his daughter. The pleasure will be great to any thoughtful man who reads the book a second time for the distinct purpose of studying its exquisite construction. Except Mr Stryver, who is necessary to the full expression of the character of Sydney Carton, and the slightly sketched family of Jerry Cruncher by the help of which Jerry himself is cunningly defined, there is not a person in the book who is not an essential portion of the story, there is not a scene that does not carry the tale onward, not even a paragraph that is not spent on urging forward the strong purpose of the book.

Mr Dickens has obtained his hold upon the public by the energy of an original genius, that penetrates with a quick instinct through the outer coverings of life to much of its essential truth. Even when he has succeeded least, the living force of a mind rarely gifted has been strongly felt. In this book all his natural powers seem to have been concentrated and directed steadily with a consummate art towards the purpose and the end it had in view. There are worse books with plots more highly wrought and exciting, deep as is the interest awakened by the *Tale of Two Cities.* In most of Mr Dickens's works there is more of the quaint humour by which his reputation was first won. Here we especially admire the energy of genius, the concentration of innumerable subtleties of thought upon a single purpose, the abiding force of the impression that is made.

The skill spent upon the depiction of the mind of Doctor Manette during the life following his release from a long burial in the Bastille it is hardly necessary to illustrate. The detail is original in its conception, yet it carries with it the conviction of deep truth. We may recal as one example of the manner of the book, the art with which the echoes of the future are suggested by the echoes in Doctor Manette's quiet street corner, near Soho square. A little group sits under the plane tree in the garden, on a sultry summer afternoon. Darnay, the future husband of Lucie, the inheritor, as it will appear, of the curse upon those by whom the Doctor had been buried alive, has by chance struck heavily upon the hidden chord that yields the key-note of the story. The Doctor starts, but refers this to one of the slight surprises against which he is not yet proof, and shows on the back of his hand that the first large drops of rain are falling. The slow coming of the storm, the hurrying of the echoes, the bursting of the tempest, blend with the innocent fancy of a girl to suggest the greater storm of which the first drops had then fallen. This is artifice, but it is the artifice of a poet, and by like touches that often are flashed suddenly into a word or through a single line, the force of poetry is added to the book. We are inevitably strengthened by a work like this, in the conviction that Mr Dickens's place hereafter in our literature will be in the first rank of the poets who have not expressed themselves in verse. 〈. . .〉

A few touches here and there may be in excess; we are hardly content, for example, that it should occur to Miss Pross, at a critical moment, to compare Madame Defarge's eyes to bed winches; but these faults, natural to an active fancy, are very few and very slight in the work now before us. It is written throughout with an energy that never wanders from its aim, a strength that uses with the subtlety of genius the resources of a studied art.

—John Forster, [Review of *A Tale of Two Cities*], *Examiner*, 10 December 1859, pp. 788–89

SIR JAMES FITZJAMES STEPHEN ON DICKENS'S CARICATURE OF HISTORY

[Sir James Fitzjames Stephen (1829–1894) was a judge, legal scholar, and literary critic. Among his major works are *A Digest of the Law of Evidence* (1876), *A Digest of the Criminal Law* (1877), and *Horae Sabbaticae* (1892), a collection of his reviews. In this review of *A Tale of Two Cities*, Stephen censures Dickens for basing his novel solely upon a reading of Carlyle's *The French Revolution* and of producing a superficial caricature of the historical period.]

The moral tone of the *Tale of Two Cities* is not more wholesome than that of its predecessors, nor does it display any nearer approach to a solid knowledge of the subject-matter to which it refers. Mr. Dickens observes in his preface—"It has been one of my hopes to add something to the popular and picturesque means of understanding that terrible time, though no one can hope to add anything to the philosophy of Mr. Carlyle's wonderful book." The allusion to Mr. Carlyle confirms the presumption which the book itself raises, that Mr. Dickens happened to have read the History of the French Revolution, and, being on the look-out for a subject, determined off-hand to write a novel about it. Whether he has any other knowledge of the subject than a single reading of Mr. Carlyle's work would supply does not appear, but certainly what he has written shows no more. It is exactly the sort of story which a man would write who had taken down Mr. Carlyle's theory without any sort of inquiry or examination, but with a comfortable conviction that "nothing could be added to its philosophy." The people, says Mr. Dickens, in effect, had been degraded by long and gross misgovernment, and acted like wild beasts in consequence. There is, no doubt, a great deal of truth in this view of the matter, but it is such very elementary truth that, unless a man had something new to say about it, it is hardly worth mentioning; and Mr. Dickens supports it by specific assertions which, if not absolutely false, are at any rate so selected as to convey an entirely false impression. It is a shameful thing for a popular writer to exaggerate the faults of the French aristocracy in a book which will naturally find its way to readers who know very little of the subject except what he chooses to tell them; but it is impossible not to feel that the melodramatic story which Mr. Dickens tells about the wicked Marquis who violates one of his serfs and murders another, is a grossly unfair representation of the state of society in France in the middle of the eighteenth century. That the French *noblesse* had much to answer for in a thousand ways, is a lamentable truth; but it is by no means true that they could rob, murder, and ravish with impunity. When Count Horn thought proper to try the experiment under the Regency, he was broken on the wheel, notwithstanding his nobility; and the sort of atrocities which Mr. Dickens depicts as characteristic of the eighteenth century were neither safe nor common in the fourteenth.

England as well as France comes in for Mr. Dickens's favours. He takes a sort of pleasure, which appears to us insolent and unbecoming in the extreme, in drawing the attention of his readers exclusively to the bad and weak points in the history and character of their immediate ancestors. The grandfathers of the present generation were, according to him, a sort of savages, or very little better. They were cruel, bigoted, unjust, ill-governed, oppressed, and neglected in every possible way. The childish delight with which Mr. Dickens acts Jack Horner, and says What a good boy am I, in comparison with my benighted ancestors, is thoroughly contemptible. England some ninety years back was not what it now is, but it was a very remarkable country. It was inhabited and passionately loved by some of the greatest men who were then living, and it possessed institutions which, with many imperfections, were by far the best which then existed in the world, and were, amongst other things, the sources from which our present liberties are derived. There certainly were a large number of abuses, but Mr. Dickens is not content with representing them fairly. He grossly exaggerates their evils. It is usually difficult to bring a novelist precisely to book, and Mr. Dickens is especially addicted to the cultivation of a judicious vagueness; but in his present work he affords an opportunity for instituting a comparison between the facts on which he relies, and the assertions which he makes on the strength of them. In the early part of his novel he introduces the trial of a man who is accused of being a French spy, and does his best to show how utterly corrupt and unfair everybody was who took part in the proceedings. The counsel for the Crown is made to praise the Government spy, who is the principal witness, as a man of exalted virtue, and is said to address himself with zeal to the task of driving the nails into the prisoner's coffin. In examining the witnesses he makes every sort of unfair suggestion which can prejudice the prisoner, and the judge shows great reluctance to allow any circumstance to come out which would be favourable to him, and does all in his power to get him hung, though the evidence against him is weak in the extreme. It so happens that in the State Trials for the very year (1780) in which the scene of Mr. Dickens's story is laid, there is a full report of the trial of a French spy—one De la Motte—for the very crime which is imputed to Mr. Dickens's hero. One of the principal witnesses in this case was an accomplice of very bad character; and in fact it is difficult to doubt that the one trial is merely a fictitious "rendering" of the other. The comparison between them is both curious and instructive. It would be perfectly impossible to imagine a fairer trial than De la Motte's, or stronger evidence than that on which he was convicted. The counsel for the Crown said not one word about the character of the approver, and so far was the judge from pressing hard on the prisoner, that he excluded evidence offered against him which in almost any other country would have been all but conclusive against him. It is surely a very disgraceful thing to represent such a transaction as an attempt to commit a judicial murder.

—Sir James Fitzjames Stephen, [Review of *A Tale of Two Cities*], *Saturday Review* (London), 17 December 1859, pp. 742–43

❖

G. K. CHESTERTON ON DICKENS'S INABILITY TO UNDERSTAND THE FRENCH

[G. K. Chesterton (1874–1936), although today best known as the author of the Father Brown detective stories, was a prolific writer on literature, religion, philosophy, and society. He had a particular affinity for Dickens, writing introductions to many of Dickens's novels (collected as *Appreciations and Criticisms of the Works of Charles Dickens,* 1911) as well as a critical study, *Charles Dickens* (1906), from which the following extract is taken. Here, Chesterton asserts that both Dickens and Carlyle, being English, were unable to understand the true motive forces behind the French Revolution.]

In dignity and eloquence ⟨*A Tale of Two Cities*⟩ almost stands alone among the books by Dickens, but it also stands alone among his books in this respect, that it is not entirely by Dickens. It owes its inspiration avowedly to the passionate and cloudy pages of Carlyle's *French Revolution.* And there is something quite essentially inconsistent between Carlyle's disturbed and half-sceptical transcendentalism and the original school and spirit to which Dickens belonged, the lucid and laughing decisiveness of the old convinced and contented Radicalism. Hence the genius of Dickens cannot save him, just as the great genius of Carlyle could not save him from making a picture of the French Revolution, which was delicately and yet deeply erroneous. Both tend too much to represent it as a mere elemental outbreak of hunger or vengeance; they do not see enough that it was a war for intellectual principles, even for intellectual platitudes. We, the modern English, cannot easily understand the French Revolution, because we cannot easily understand the idea of bloody battle for pure common sense; we cannot understand common sense in arms and conquering. In modern England common sense appears to mean putting up with existing conditions. For us a practical politician really means a man who can be thoroughly trusted to do nothing at all; that is where his practicality comes in. The French feeling— the feeling at the back of the Revolution—was that the more sensible a man was, the more you must look out for slaughter.

In all the imitators of Carlyle, including Dickens, there is an obscure sentiment that the thing for which the Frenchmen died must have been something new and queer, a paradox, a strange idolatry. But when such blood ran in the streets, it was for the sake of a truism; when those cities were shaken to their foundations, they were shaken to their foundations by a truism.

I have mentioned this historical matter because it illustrates these later and more mingled influences which at once improve and as it were perplex the later work of Dickens. For Dickens had in his original mental composition capacities for understanding this cheery and sensible element in the French Revolution far better than Carlyle. The French Revolution was, among other things, French, and, so far as that goes, could never have a precise counterpart in so jolly and autochthonous an Englishman as Charles Dickens. But there was a great deal of the actual and unbroken tradition of the Revolution itself in his early radical indictments; in his denunciations of the Fleet Prison there was a great deal of the capture of the Bastille. There was, above all, a certain reasonable impatience which was the essence of the old Republican, and which is quite unknown to the Revolutionist in modern Europe. The old Radical did not feel exactly that he was "in revolt;" he felt if anything that a number of idiotic institutions had revolted against reason and against him. Dickens, I say, had the revolutionary idea, though an English form of it, by clear and conscious inheritance; Carlyle had to rediscover the Revolution by a violence of genius and vision. If Dickens, then, took from Carlyle (as he said he did) his image of the Revolution, it does certainly mean that he had forgotten something of his own youth and come under the more complex influences of the end of the nineteenth century.

—G. K. Chesterton, *Charles Dickens* (New York: Dodd, Mead, 1906), pp. 233–36

ARTHUR WAUGH ON DICKENS'S TIGHTNESS OF CONSTRUCTION

[Arthur Waugh (1866–1943), aside from writing studies of Alfred, Lord Tennyson (1892) and Robert Browning (1900), was for many years the managing director of Dickens's original publisher, Chapman & Hall, about which Waugh wrote a memoir, *A Hundred Years of Publishing* (1930). In this extract, Waugh believes *A Tale of Two Cities* to foreshadow Dickens's later work in being tightly constructed in its plot and incidents.]

There is a letter from Dickens to Bulwer Lytton, written in June, 1860, which is of considerable interest as showing the care with which the author had worked up the historical portions of the story. Lytton had apparently criticized the lack of perspective in the relation between the old marquis and his peasants, objecting that such atrocities had certainly not occurred so closely in point of time to the Reign of Terror as Dickens's narrative suggested. To this, Dickens replied that he had "many reasons to believe that some of the (feudal) privileges had been used to the frightful oppression of the peasant, quite as near to the time of the Revolution as the Doctor's narrative, which dates long before the Terror." He added, "There is a curious book printed at Amsterdam, written to make out no case whatever, and tiresome enough in its literal dictionary-like minuteness; scattered up and down the pages of which is full authority for my marquis. This is Mercier's Tableau de Paris. Rousseau is the authority for the peasant's shutting up his house when he had a bit of meat. The tax-taker was the authority for the wretched creature's imprisonment." The same letter defends the author from a charge of inartistic impropriety in letting Madame Defarge's death be the work of chance. "Where the accident is inseparable from the passion and action of the character; where it is strictly consistent with the entire design, and arises out of some culminating proceeding on the part of the individual which the whole story had led up to; it seems to me to become, as it were, an act of divine justice. And when I use Miss Pross (though this is quite another question) to bring about such a catastrophe, I have the positive intention of making that half-comic intervention a part of the desperate woman's failure; and of opposing that mean death, instead of a desperate one in the streets, which she wouldn't have minded, to the dignity of Carton's. Wrong or right, this was all design, and seemed to me to be in the fitness of things."

This will seem to most people good criticism and illuminative. There is one other fact in connection with *A Tale of Two Cities* which invites commemoration; perhaps, even, without too curious an inquiry, it may be said to fall, fittingly enough, into its position in the story of Dickens's life. If *Little Dorrit* may be described as a novel of farewells, *A Tale of Two Cities* may, with equal propriety, be called a story of new departures. It was connected in Dickens's life with the story of a parting which coloured all that remained to him of length of days and activity; it marks, in the story of his art, a new departure upon the path of incident and construction. Henceforth the old form of leisurely narrative was never to be returned to. *Great Expectations* is as much a story of incident, "pounding out its characters in a mortar" as *A Tale of Two Cities* itself; and though *Our Mutual Friend* comes nearer to the old method, it is much more deliberately incidental than even *Bleak House.* The construction of a plot, the weaving of a narrative have now become the absorbing interests of Dickens's art; and there are many who believe that, had his last unfinished book received his final touches, it would have been the best-constructed and the most incidental of them all.

—Arthur Waugh, "Introducing *A Tale of Two Cities,*" *Dickensian* 23 (1927): 14–15

GEORGE ORWELL ON DICKENS'S AMBIVALENT ATTITUDE TOWARD THE FRENCH REVOLUTION

[George Orwell (1903–1950), the pseudonym of the British writer Eric Blair, is best known for the novels *Animal Farm* (1945) and *Nineteen Eighty-four* (1949), but he was also a penetrating critic and reviewer. In this extract, from his lengthy essay on Dickens, Orwell claims that Dickens's attitude toward the French Revolution was ambivalent: Although he felt that the aristocracy deserved what it got for its oppression of the peasantry, he also believed that the Revolution and its excesses was something that might have been avoided.]

The one thing that everyone who has read *A Tale of Two Cities* remembers is the Reign of Terror. The whole book is dominated by the guillotine—tumbrils thundering to and fro, bloody knives, heads bouncing into the basket, and sinister old women knitting as they watch. Actually these scenes only occupy a few chapters, but they are written with terrible intensity, and the rest of the book is rather slow going. But *A Tale of Two Cities* is not a companion volume to *The Scarlet Pimpernel*. Dickens sees clearly enough that the French Revolution was bound to happen and that many of the people who were executed deserved what they got. If, he says, you behave as the French aristocracy had behaved, vengeance will follow. He repeats this over and over again. We are constantly being reminded that while "my lord" is lolling in bed, with four liveried footmen serving his chocolate and the peasants starving outside, somewhere in the forest a tree is growing which will presently be sawn into planks for the platform of the guillotine, etc etc etc. The inevitability of the Terror, given its causes, is insisted upon the clearest terms. ⟨. . .⟩

In other words, the French aristocracy had dug their own graves. But there is no perception here of what is now called historic necessity. Dickens sees that the results are inevitable, given the causes, but he thinks that the causes might have been avoided. The Revolution is something that happens because centuries of oppression have made the French peasantry sub-human. If the wicked nobleman could somehow have turned over a new leaf, like Scrooge, there would have been no Revolution, no *jacquerie,* no guillotine—and so much the better. This is the opposite of the "revolutionary" attitude. From the "revolutionary" point of view the class-struggle is the main source of progress, and therefore the nobleman who robs the peasant and goads him to revolt is playing a necessary part, just as much as the Jacobin who guillotines the nobleman. Dickens never writes anywhere a line that can be interpreted as meaning this. Revolution as he sees it is merely a monster that is begotten by tyranny and always ends by devouring its own instruments. In Sydney Carton's vision at the foot of the guillotine, he foresees Defarge and the other leading spirits of the Terror all perishing under the same knife—which, in fact, was approximately what happened.

And Dickens is very sure that revolution *is* a monster. That is why everyone remembers the revolutionary scenes in *A Tale of Two Cities;* they have the quality of nightmare, and it is Dickens's own nightmare. Again and again he insists upon the meaningless horrors of revolution—the mass-butcheries, the injustice, the ever-present terror of spies, the frightful bloodlust of the mob. The descriptions of the Paris mob—the description, for instance, of the crowd of murderers struggling round the grindstone to sharpen their weapons before butchering the prisoners in the September massacres—outdo anything in *Barnaby Rudge.* The revolutionaries appear to him simply as degraded savages—in fact, as lunatics. He broods over their frenzies with a curious imaginative intensity. ⟨. . .⟩ Madame Defarge is a truly dreadful figure, certainly Dickens's most successful attempt at a *malignant* character. Defarge and others are simply "the new oppressors who have risen on the destruction of the old", the revolutionary courts are presided over by "the lowest, cruellest and worst populace", and so on and so forth. All, the way through Dickens insists upon the nightmare insecurity of a revolutionary period, and in this he shows a great deal of prescience. "A law of the suspected, which struck away all security for liberty or life, and delivered over any good and innocent person to any bad and guilty one; prisons gorged with people who had committed no offence, and could obtain no hearing"—it would apply pretty accurately to several countries today.

The apologists of any revolution generally try to minimise its horrors; Dickens's impulse is to exaggerate them—and from a historical point of view he has certainly exaggerated. Even the Reign of Terror was a much smaller thing than he makes it appear. Though he quotes no figures, he gives the impression of a frenzied massacre lasting for years, whereas in reality the whole of the Terror, so far as the number of deaths goes, was a joke compared with one of Napoleon's battles. But the bloody knives and the tumbrils rolling to and fro create in his mind a special, sinister vision which he has succeeded in passing on to generations of readers. Thanks to Dickens, the very word "tumbril" has a murderous sound; one forgets that a tumbril is only a sort of farm-cart. To this day, to the average Englishman, the French Revolution means no more than a pyramid of severed heads. It is a strange thing that Dickens, much more in sympathy with the ideas of the Revolution than most Englishmen of his time, should have played a part in creating this impression.

—George Orwell, "Charles Dickens" (1939), *Dickens, Dali and Others* (Harcourt, Brace & World, 1946), pp. 12–16

JACK LINDSAY ON THE INFLUENCE OF BULWER-LYTTON ON DICKENS

[Jack Lindsay (1900–1990), a prolific British novelist, historian, biographer, translator, and classical scholar, wrote such works as *Charles Dickens: A Biographical and Critical Study* (1950), *After the 'Thirties: The Novel in Britain and Its Future* (1956), and *William Blake: His Life and Work* (1978). In this extract, Lindsay traces the influence of the novel *Zanoni* (1842) by Edward Bulwer-Lytton (1803–1873) on *A Tale of Two Cities,* showing that Dickens adopted the basic symbolic framework of Bulwer-Lytton's work for his own.]

In seeking the spiritual impacts behind any turn of development in Dickens it is always safe to look at Bulwer-Lytton's work; for that writer throughout his novels drew powerfully on certain traditional imagery, carried on from folk-days in various forms of popular or semi-popular expression. He influenced Dickens at decisive moments again and again: for example, his *Paul Clifford* led on to *Oliver Twist,* his *Night and Morning* led on to *Martin Chuzzlewit.* The work of his which underlay *A Tale of Two Cities* was *Zanoni* (1842).

Zanoni's method links closely with that of *A Tale.* Bulwer is openly writing a symbolic account of the creative process, in which all the characters, one way or another, represent phases or forms, types or anti-types, of the creator in his movement to enlarged or constricted life. This method is more rationalized in *A Tale,* but it is present in a degree that Dickens would scarcely have reached without knowing Bulwer's book. Further *Zanoni* takes the French Revolution as its scene, to merge the personally creative struggle with a social convulsion of change.

Dickens revives his memory of *Zanoni* because he now feels the need to grapple with his pangs of consciousness in a related way. Inevitably he brings the method down to earth more than Bulwer, and to some extent changes the method of symbolic representations into one of dramatic realization. But the travail of his spirit appears in the extent to which the allegorical substratum intrudes and prevents a fully concrete character-projection.

Bulwer's attitude is far from that of Carlyle. With his odd kind of Tory anarchism he politically abhors the Revolution and tries consciously to reduce it to a demented terrorism. But in the working-out of his allegory he cannot help giving it further values, which in the end achieve something like a full acceptance of its action at deeper levels than those of intellectual judgment. For, if the Revolution is the moment when the creative process reaches its intensest moment of conflict and union (as *Zanoni* implies), then the schematic political attitude falls away and sets free a quite different conception, in which revolution and stability, death and life, are equally accepted as aspects of process.

Zanoni, the idealizing and integrating art-activity, is opposed to old Melnour, the contemplative and analytic mind. But both these figures are opposed in turn to Glyndon, emblem of art-science which strives to rise above convention and stereotype, but is stricken down by the attack of fear on the threshold of adventure into the unknown (the human future, the unconscious). Both Glyndon and Zanoni compete for possession of Viola (love, the affective life, union); and the spiritual drama of their struggles is linked throughout with the tumults and clashes of the Revolution. Bulwer, despite his hectic denunciations of the Terror, finds himself willynilly in the position of identifying the innermost struggle of human and artistic values with the struggle of basic social change.

His Viola is arrested in Paris at the height of the Terror (through the jealous hauntings of Nicot and Fillide). Glyndon, whose contact with her was the direct cause of her danger, has fled; but Zanoni steps in and substitutes himself for her on the guillotine.

The derivation of *A Tale* from *Zanoni* is certain; for it appears both in method and theme. But in the years between 1842 and 1859, Dickens's mind has transmuted *Zanoni's* tensions and forms into something very different. The frankly and wildly symbolic tale has been rationalized and psychologized, but the undissolved structure is visible. Dickens like Bulwer wants to define the crucial moment of personal pang and growth in terms of the revolutionary situation and to find by these means the clue to human and artistic growth. In Bulwer the emblem of new life is the Child, in Dickens it is the United Lovers. In Bulwer Zanoni must sacrifice himself to save the new life, because the idealizing activity has gone too far and has lost human sympathy; and Glyndon must flee, because he is the artist who cannot break through his fear into a renewal of art and life. But the total effect of all the unions and cleavages, possessions and renunciations, is to liberate the creative image, to beget the child. Out of the revolutionary pangs of birth comes the continuity of life, the fresh stabilization of the life-process. ⟨. . .⟩

In *A Tale,* with its less obvious allegory, and its more direct acceptance of social process, the romantic formulas of lovers-restored-to-one-another and the defeated-curse are used, and it is the rejected or excluded one who makes the sacrifice. But however differently the ingredients are mixed, the kinship of pattern remains; and a consideration of *Zanoni* helps us much further to an understanding of the passionate moment when Dickens felt that at last he could and must use the French Revolution as material and setting for a novel.

—Jack Lindsay, "*A Tale of Two Cities*," *Life and Letters* 62, No. 3 (September 1949): 197–200

❖

MONROE ENGEL ON PERSONAL REGENERATION IN *A TALE OF TWO CITIES*

[Monroe Engel (b. 1921), a former professor of English at Harvard University, is a novelist as well as the author of *The Maturity of Dickens* (1959), from which the following extract is taken. Here, Engel believes the central theme of *A Tale of Two Cities* is personal regeneration, or the notion of a resurrection from a state of near-death.]

In the very first chapter, the message that Mr. Lorry has Jerry Cruncher convey back to Tellson's is "RECALLED TO LIFE." Dr. Manette is in fact recalled to life from a living death into which he can relapse under sufficient strain, and which for many years at least he can only stave off with an effort that he cannot even relinquish when he sleeps. Darnay too, in prison, thinks " 'Now am I left, as if I were dead.' Stopping then, to look down at the mattress, he turned from it with a sick feeling, and thought 'And here in these crawling creatures is the first condition of the body after death.' "

Sidney Carton tells Lucy Manette that he is "like one who died young. All my life might have been." His life having been a kind of death, it is appropriate that his death should be the beginning of his life and that he should die repeating Christ's promise to Martha of resurrection for the faithful. A comic rendering of the same theme is provided by Jerry Cruncher, who by night plies the trade of "Resurrection Man," and who is led by self-interest to the conviction that though it's "hard enough" of the law to execute a criminal, it's "wery hard" to quarter him and thereby "spile him." In this same comic exploitation of the theme of regeneration or resurrection, the spy Cly is the false Lazarus, who has risen from his grave easily enough because he has never been placed in it, and who has been saved from death by his simulated burial.

The theme of personal regeneration has the utmost pertinence for the general or historical meaning of a novel that testifies to the sufficient and miserable causes for revolution, but in which revolution itself accomplishes and is capable of accomplishing nothing but butchery, aggravating rather than relieving misery. Defarge comforts the father of the child killed by the Marquis's carriage by telling him that it is "better for the poor little plaything to die so, than to live. It has died in a moment without pain. Could it have lived an hour as happily?" This is the much reiterated statement of *Bleak House,* which concerns itself also with redemption. The brother of the girl whom the Marquis's brother has forced to become his mistress summons the Marquis and all his "bad race" to answer for their crimes in "the days when all these things are to be answered for"; and Doctor Manette ends his testament with the same summons.

The condition of the French people prior to the Revolution is pictured as a terrestrial hell—the condition ascribed to life more or less consistently in all the novels of Dickens' maturity, but with great literalness here. An extraordinary number of the French scenes, starting properly with the very first French scene, of the bloody wine spilled in the streets, are infernal. This hellishness is in substantial part man-made, the result of injustice and oppression. But Dickens is never sentimental about the victims of oppression. No transfer of power will change hell to heaven, for the plague of "the frightful moral disorder" has corrupted oppressors and oppressed equally, if not uniformly. The only genuine answer is both distant and radical, a profound regeneration of the human spirit. In this sense, the novel is a tale not so much of two cities as of all places, and it is possibly the great appeal of the theme of regeneration that makes this thin and often mawkish novel far more widely read than are most of the better novels Dickens wrote.

—Monroe Engel, *The Maturity of Dickens* (Cambridge, MA: Harvard University Press, 1959), pp. 178–80

JOHN GROSS ON CARTON AND DARNAY

[John Gross (b. 1935), an editorial consultant for the *Observer* (London) and a member of the editorial staff of the *New York Times Book Review,* has written critical studies of John P. Marquand (1963) and James Joyce (1970) as well as *The Rise and Fall of the Man of Letters* (1969). In this extract, Gross maintains that *A Tale of Two Cities* is structured around the figures of Carton and Darnay, who respectively represent the wastrel and the hero in the novel.]

A Tale of Two Cities is a tale of two heroes. The theme of the double has such obvious attractions for a writer preoccupied with disguises, rival impulses, and hidden affinities that it is surprising that Dickens didn't make more use of it elsewhere. But no one could claim that his handling of the device is very successful here, or that he has managed to range the significant forces of the novel behind Carton and Darnay. Darnay is, so to speak, the accredited representative of Dickens in the novel, the 'normal' hero for whom a happy ending is still possible. It has been noted, interestingly enough, that he shares his creator's initials—and that is pretty well the only interesting thing about him. Otherwise he is a pasteboard character, completely undeveloped. His position as an exile, his struggles as a language-teacher, his admiration for George Washington are so many openings thrown away.

Carton, of course, is a far more striking figure. He belongs to the line of cultivated wastrels who play an increasingly large part in Dickens's novels during the second half of his career, culminating in Eugene Wrayburn; his clearest predecessor, as his name indicates, is the luckless Richard Carstone of *Bleak House.* He has squandered his gifts and drunk away his early promise; his will is broken, but his intellect is unimpaired. In a sense, his opposite is not Darnay at all, but the aggressive Stryver, who makes a fortune by picking his brains. Yet there is something hollow about his complete resignation to failure: his self-abasement in front of Lucie, for instance. ('I am like one who died young . . . I know very well that you can have no tenderness for me . . .') For, stagy a figure though he is, Carton does suggest what Thomas Hardy calls 'fearful unfulfilments'; he still has vitality, and it is hard to believe that he has gone down without a struggle. The total effect is one of energy held unnaturally in check: the bottled-up frustration which Carton represents must spill over somewhere.

Carton's and Darnay's fates are entwined from their first meeting, at the Old Bailey trial. Over the dock there hangs a mirror: 'crowds of the wicked and the wretched had been reflected in it, and had passed from its surface and this earth's together. Haunted in a most ghastly manner that abominable place would have been, if the glass could ever have rendered back its reflections, as the ocean is one day to give up its dead.' (Bk. II, Ch. 2.) After Darnay's acquittal we leave him with Carton, 'so like each other in feature, so unlike in manner, both reflected in the glass above them'. Reflections, like ghosts, suggest unreality and self-division, and at the end of the same day Carton stares at his own image in the glass and upbraids it: 'Why should you particularly like a man who resembles you? There is nothing in you to like: you know that. Ah, confound you! . . . Come on, and have it out in plain words! You hate the fellow.' (Bk. II, Ch. 4.) In front of the mirror, Carton thinks of changing places with Darnay; at the end of the book, he is to take the other's death upon him. Dickens prepares the ground: when Darnay is in jail, it is Carton who strikes Mr. Lorry as having 'the wasted air of a prisoner', and when he is visited by Carton on the rescue attempt, he thinks at first that he is 'an apparition of his own imagining'. But Dickens is determined to stick by Darnay: a happy ending *must* be possible. As Lorry and his party gallop to safety with the drugged Darnay, there is an abrupt switch to the first person: 'The wind is rushing after us, and the clouds are flying after us, and the moon is plunging after us, and the whole wild night is in pursuit of us; but so far, we are pursued by nothing else.' (Bk. III, Ch. 13.) *We* can make our escape, however narrowly; Carton, expelled from our system, must be abandoned to his fate.

But the last word is with Carton—the most famous last word in Dickens, in fact. Those who take a simplified view of Dickens's radicalism, or regard him as one of nature's Marxists, can hardly help regretting that *A Tale of Two Cities* should end as it does. They are bound to feel, with Edgar Johnson, that 'instead of merging, the truth of revolution and the truth of sacrifice are made to appear in conflict'. A highly personal, indeed a unique crisis cuts across public issues and muffles the political message. But this is both to sentimentalize Dickens's view of the revolution, and to miss the point about Carton. The cynical judgment that his sacrifice was trifling, since he had nothing to live for, is somewhat nearer the mark. Drained of the will to live, he is shown in the closing chapters of the book as a man courting death, and embracing it when it comes. 'In seasons of pestilence, some of us will have a secret attraction to the disease—a terrible passing inclination to die of it. And all of us have like wonders hidden in our breasts, only needing circumstances to evoke them.' (Bk. III, Ch. 6.) It is Carton rather than Darnay who is 'drawn to the loadstone rock.' On his last walk around Paris, a passage which Shaw cites in the preface to *Man and Superman* as proof of Dickens's essentially irreligious nature, his thoughts run on religion: 'I am the Resurrection and the Life.' But his impressions are all of death: the day comes coldly, 'looking like a dead face out of the sky', while on the river 'a trading boat, with a sail of the softened colour of a dead leaf, then glided into his view, floated by him, and died away'. (Bk. III, Ch. 9.) His walk recalls an earlier night, when he wandered round London with 'wreaths of dust spinning round and round before the morning blast, as if the desert sand had risen far away and the first spray of it in its advance had begun to overwhelm the city'. (Bk. II, Ch. 5.) Then, with the wilderness bringing home to him a sense of the wasted powers within him, he saw a momentary mirage of what he might have achieved and was reduced to tears; but now that the city has been overwhelmed in earnest, he is past thinking of what might have been. 'It is a far, far better thing that I do, than I have ever done'—but the 'better thing' might just as well be committing suicide as laying down his life for Darnay. At any rate, he thinks of himself as going towards rest, not towards resurrection.

—John Gross, "A Tale of Two Cities," Dickens and the Twentieth Century, ed. John Gross and Gabriel Pearson (London: Routledge & Kegan Paul, 1962), pp. 189–92

EARLE DAVIS ON CARLYLE'S INFLUENCE ON DICKENS

[Earle Davis (b. 1905), a former professor of English at Kansas State University, is the author of *Vision Fugitive: Ezra Pound and Economics* (1968) and *The Flint and the Flame: The Artistry of Charles Dickens* (1963), from which the following extract is taken. Here, Davis studies the number of features Dickens has derived directly from Carlyle's *The French Revolution*.]

Defarge and his wife come indirectly from Carlyle. The history presents Santerre, a brewer, living in Saint-Antoine, who became a leader of the revolt, and Carlyle makes casual mention of the president of the Jacobin Society, whose name was Lafarge. A certain Usher Maillard was active in the storming of the Bastille, doing most of what Defarge did in Dickens' narrative. "Defarge" combines from these originals whatever the novelist needed for his action. Carlyle also devoted eleven chapters in his history of the early rioting to "The Insurrection of the Women." One of his female leaders, a black Joan of Arc, was Demoiselle Théroigne, a striking and spectacular mob captain. In the fight at the Tuileries, Carlyle describes her as *Sibyl* Théroigne: "Vengeance, *Victoire ou la mort!*" Mme. Defarge is not "small-waisted," but she performs as mob leader, being much more ruthless than her husband. Dickens also invents a character, a companion of Mme. Defarge, whom he designates only as The Vengeance. He took what he wanted from Carlyle, changed and concentrated it, and dressed up the details of his story from the historical record.

Carlyle attributes the worst excesses of the mob to the Jacobins, or the *Jacquerie*. Dickens creates types of revolt leaders from the lowest classes, giving them the names of Jacques One, Jacques Two, Jacques Three. The insignia of the French Revolution was patterned in threes—witness the tricolor and the slogan, "Liberty, Fraternity, and Equality." The Jacobin women were especially prominent at the guillotine, too, and the stories of their knitting while watching the executions were famous. Carlyle describes them at the executions, and Dickens applies this graphic bit of data to Mme. Defarge's knitted record of victims, handwork in which the names of the doomed were entwined with vengeance in her own variety of shorthand. The women are there knitting when Carton dies.

Names occasionally wander from one book to the other, perhaps in some entirely different connection from the original, showing merely that the name remained in Dickens' mind and was appropriated because the novelist needed some kind of cognomen. The hated *gabelle,* France's salt tax, turns up as the name of Darnay's agent on Monseigneur's estate, the man whose letter to Darnay begging his assistance in his trial is the excuse for tempting Darnay back to France and his capture. Carlyle casually mentions Thelusson's Bank, where the great Necker was once a clerk. Dickens, needing a name for the agency which served to bring Lucy Manette and later her father from France to England, shifted the establishment to Tellson's Bank, with branches in Paris as well as London.

Carlyle's description of the butchery which went on outside La Force Prison in the September Massacres of 1792 is about as horrible as anything in his chamber of hyperbolic horrors. Wanton and brutal slaying in the streets with axe and sword is much more forthright than death under the guillotine. Dickens describes the great grindstone in the yard outside the quarters of Tellson's Bank in Paris where the mob, shirts and clothing dripping with the blood of their victims, comes to sharpen weapons blunted in the awful slaughter.

Much of this transposition is the routine custom of the historical novelist, taking his details from a reputable source and supplying his facts where they are needed in his story. Of more interest to the critic of narrative technique are the instances in which only a suggestion is in the source, Dickens' expansion adding to the picture or the characterization which becomes an important part of his story. Dr. Manette, for example, lost his mind in the long years of confinement. He learned the shoemaker's trade in prison, and although nursed back to health and sanity upon coming to England, he suffers lapses of memory and reverts to his prison occupation whenever he is seriously troubled. This regression happens when Lucy marries Darnay and again when all seems lost and Darnay is sentenced to die.

—Earle Davis, *The Flint and the Flame: The Artistry of Charles Dickens* (Columbia: University of Missouri Press, 1963), pp. 247–48

ROBERT ALTER ON VIOLENCE IN *A TALE OF TWO CITIES*

[Robert Alter (b. 1935) is a widely published critic and the author of *Fielding and the Nature of the Novel* (1968), *The Pleasures of Reading in an Ideological Age* (1989), and several books on the Bible and on American Jewish literature. He is a professor of Hebrew and comparative literature at the University of California at Berkeley. In this extract, Alter asserts that, although Dickens attempted to portray the potential of human regeneration in *A Tale of Two Cities*, it is the many scenes of revolutionary violence that remain most clearly in our minds.]

What Dickens is ultimately concerned with in *A Tale of Two Cities* is not a particular historical event—that is simply his chosen dramatic setting—but rather the relationship between history and evil, how violent oppression breeds violent rebellion which becomes a new kind of oppression. His account of the *ancien régime* and the French Revolution is a study in civilized man's vocation for proliferating moral chaos, and in this one important regard the *Tale* is the most compelling "modern" of his novels. He also tries hard, through the selfless devotion of his more exemplary characters, to suggest something of mankind's potential for moral regeneration; but he is considerably less convincing in this effort, partly because history itself offers so little evidence which the imagination of hope can use to sustain itself.

The most powerful imaginings of the novel reach out again and again to touch ultimate possibilities of violence, whether in the tidal waves of mass destruction or in the hideous inventiveness of individual acts of cruelty. In the first chapter we are introduced to France through the detailed description of an execution by horrible mutilation, and to England by a rapid series of images of murder, mob violence, and hangings. Throughout the novel, the English mob is in potential what the French revolutionary hordes are in bloody fact. At the English trial of the falsely accused Darnay, the "ogreish" spectators, eagerly awaiting the condemnation, vie with one another in their lip-smacking description of how a man looks being drawn and quartered. Again in France, the details of torture and savagery exercise an obscure fascination over the imagination of the characters (and perhaps of the writer as well)—nightmarish images of tongues torn out with pincers, gradual dismemberment, boiling oil and lead poured into gaping wounds, float through the darkness of the novel and linger on the retina of the memory.

The energy of destruction that gathers to such acts of concentrated horror pulses through the whole world of the novel, pounding at its foundations. It is conceived as an elemental force in nature which works through men as well. Dover Beach as Jarvis Lorry contemplates it near the beginning of the novel is a replica in nature of the revolution to come, the scene most strikingly serving as event: "the sea did what it liked, and what it liked was destruction. It thundered at the town, and thundered at the cliffs, and brought the coast down madly." The image of the revolutionary mob, much later in the novel, is simply the obverse of this vision of the ocean as chaos and darkness: "The sea of black and threatening waters, and of destructive upheaving of wave against wave, whose depths were yet unfathomed and whose forces were yet unknown. The remorseless sea of turbulently swaying shapes, voices of vengeance." These same pitiless forces are present in the rainstorm that descends upon the quiet Soho home of the Manettes as Lucie, Darnay, and Carton watch: the lightning, harbinger of revolution, that they see leaping from the stormy dark is the only light that can be born from the murky atmosphere of this world—the hot light of destruction. Later the revolution is also likened to a great earthquake, and when Madame Defarge adds to this her grim declaration—"Tell wind and fire where to stop . . . but don't tell me"—all four elements of the traditional world-picture have been associated with the forces of blind destruction, earth and water and fire and air.

There is, ultimately, a peculiar impersonality about this novel, for it is intended to dramatize the ways in which human beings become the slaves of impersonal forces, at last are made inhuman by them. In order to show the play of these elemental forces in history, Dickens adopts a generalizing novelistic technique which frequently approaches allegory, the mode of imagination traditionally used for the representation of cosmic powers doing battle or carrying out a destined plan. The Darkness and Light of the novel's first sentence are almost immediately supported by the introduction of two explicitly allegorical figures in the same chapter: the Woodman, Fate; and the Farmer, Death. In the action that follows, events and characters often assume the symbolic postures and formal masks of allegory.

—Robert Alter, "The Demons of History in Dickens's *Tale*" (1969), *Motives for Fiction* (Cambridge, MA: Harvard University Press, 1984), pp. 106–8

SYLVÈRE MONOD ON *A TALE OF TWO CITIES* AS CHARACTERISTIC OF DICKENS'S WORK

[Sylvère Monod (b. 1921), a former professor of English at the Sorbonne in Paris, is a leading scholar on Dickens. He has written *Dickens the Novelist* (1968) and a study, *Martin Chuzzlewit* (1985), and (with George Lord) has edited *Hard Times* (1966) and *Bleak House* (1977). In this extract, Monod ruminates over how characteristic *A Tale of Two Cities* is of Dickens's work as a whole, finding more humor in it than many scholars have done but also finding unreality, theatricality, and melodrama.]

One of the great debates about *A Tale of Two Cities* is as to how far one finds the genuine Dickens in it. The touchstone of the genuine Dickens is comic characterization. The debate soon narrows down to the simpler question about Jerry Cruncher as a comic or even a humorous figure. I have been repeatedly charged with failing—probably because I am a Frenchman—to appreciate Jerry. But I derive some comfort from the company in which I find myself, a distinguished and by no means unduly Gallic group. Apart from Bernard Darwin (who, after nearly confessing that the *Tale* "is not quite the genuine Dickens," adds "but let us not forget Jerry Cruncher, who is the real thing"), most of the critics have been in agreement on that point, from John Forster to John Gross, and Edgar Johnson, who finds much to admire in the *Tale* and has written eloquently about it, sees only "the smallest glints of comedic exception" to the general seriousness of the novel. It is only fair to add that, on being sent back to the book with a guilty conscience, under the impression that I had not done full justice to its merits or to its mirth, I again found that its humor comes only in driblets, but that they are more numerous and pleasurable than I had remembered. Darnay's English trial (II, iii) is a great comic success. Stryver, in spite of his limited psychological range and of the author's excessive dislike of him, provides excellent opportunity for comedy and for grotesque exaggeration, for example, in II, xii, his bursting out of the Bank caused "such a concussion of air on his passage through, that to stand up against it, bowing behind two counters, required the utmost remaining strength of the two ancient clerks." Jerry himself, after all, achieves the very unusual feat of being more funny after his conversion (III, ix) than he was as a rogue. His famous—or infamous—repetition of "flopping" to describe his wife's praying even makes good in the end, since its being used in conversation with Miss Pross leads to that lady's comment, "Whatever housekeeping arrangement that may be, . . . I have no doubt it is best that Mrs. Cruncher should have it entirely under her own superintendence" (III, xiv). This is unsensational, this is tame, and one may question the legitimacy of that kind of built-in humor which rests on the use of esoteric phrases by the characters. Miss Pross herself is in the tradition of Dickens' large-hearted eccentrics, of his gruff diamonds, like Miss Betsey of whom she is somewhat reminiscent (II, vi, "Hundreds of People"); such comparisons are, of course, damning with faint praise, for it cannot be contended that Miss Pross rises to the superb comic wealth of Miss Trotwood. However, one may penitently admit that humor in *A Tale of Two Cities* is not non-existent, although irony, both under Carlyle's influence and as an effect of Dickens' own polemical purpose here, is much more abundant.

Unfortunately, other usual Dickensian characteristics are also perceptibly present in the book. Pathos and unreality are indeed all too evident: the dying words of the Darnay's little son, spoken "with a radiant smile . . . in a halo on a pillow" (II, xxi), are more than most readers can take. Lucie Manette's introduction to her father (I, vi) rings disastrously false and has all the usual features—such as exclamation, repetition, and capitalization—with which Em'ly's letters to her uncle had long ago familiarized Dickens' readers. Similar lapses into unreality are observable whenever edifying emotion is attempted; any comment on the stylistic devices in chapter ii of book III, for instance, is discouraged by the utter lack of verisimilitude in the words exchanged by the Darnays. The love-scenes (II, x, and II, xiii) are likewise drearily platitudinous, although the gestures are sometimes (in II, xiii, at any rate) less feeble than the speeches. As for theatricality and melodrama, two of the novelist's besetting sins, the ways in which they overshadow many passages of the *Tale* has often been denounced. The dramatic origin of the book, conceived while Dickens was acting in *The Frozen Deep,* has something to do with this, as also the fact that the *Tale* was the first novel written since the inception of the public readings.

—Sylvère Monod, "Some Stylistic Devices in *A Tale of Two Cities," Dickens the Craftsman: Strategies of Presentation,* ed. Robert B. Partlow, Jr. (Carbondale: Southern Illinois University Press, 1970), pp. 168–70

❖

[Edwin M. Eigner (b. 1931) is a former professor of English at the University of California at Riverside and the author of *The Metaphysical Novel in England and America* (1978) and *The Dickens Pantomime* (1989). In this extract, taken from an issue of *Dickens Studies Annual* largely devoted to *A Tale of Two Cities,* Eigner studies the figure of Darnay, finding him not fully filling the role of a Revolutionary hero because Dickens himself did not believe in such a figure.]

⟨. . .⟩ how much of Charles Darnay's guilt is not only an expression of the condition of man after the Fall and of undeniable psychological trauma, but is caused and perhaps justified by Charles's failures as social man?

To begin with, he has not fulfilled the first charge of his life, to sell his mother's jewels and give the money to the sister of the raped peasant girl, Madame Defarge, as it turns out. In fact, we are not told that Charles so much as made an attempt at carrying out this obligation, although it is possible that this is what he was trying to do on those mysterious trips between England and France between 1775 and 1780. This is special pleading in Charles's behalf, for there is no evidence, but I can think of no other explanation for the secrecy of these journeys, a secrecy which, at his English trial for treason, Charles maintains at very serious expense to his case and danger to his life. He told Lucie he "was travelling under an assumed name" because he "was travelling on a business of a delicate and difficult nature, which might get people into trouble." He could not have been divesting himself of his estate, for he had not come into that yet, and it is difficult to imagine who, besides himself and anti-aristocratic agents helping in the search for the wronged girl, might be in any danger. Still it is curious that *Dickens* maintains the secrecy, and curious also that Darnay, usually so apt to feel guilty, does not torture himself about this failure to carry out his mother's first command.

On the other hand, Darnay is distraught at his powerlessness to, as he says, "execute the last request of my dear mother's lips, and obey the last look of my dear mother's eyes, which implored me to have mercy and to redress." The powerlessness comes, presumably, from Charles's situation of having been passed over in the inheritance—his wicked uncle rules instead of him—but when he does succeed to the estate, just hours after making this speech, he is still unable to perform effectively:

> he had acted imperfectly. He knew very well, that in his love for Lucie, his renunciation of his social place, though by no means new to his mind, had been hurried and incomplete. He knew that he ought to have systematically worked it out and supervised it, and that he had meant to do it, and that it had never been done. . . . he had watched the times for a time of action . . . until the time had gone by.

But even this confession of failure by Charles misses the point. Presumably his mother's lips and eyes had not implored him to renounce his power, but rather to use it for the sake of the poor.

Nevertheless, the sense of guilt and shame called up by this train of thought impels Charles's return to France for the sake of saving his servant and using his influence to moderate the revolution. Dickens writes "His latent uneasiness had been, that bad aims were being worked out in his own unhappy land by bad instruments, and that he, who could not fail to know that he was better than they, was not there, trying to do something to stay the bloodshed, and assert the claims of mercy and humanity." All very fine, but painful though it is to contradict T. A. Jackson, perhaps the one critic who has something positive to say about Charles, I am not sure Dickens wants us entirely to admire the "large-hearted generosity" of his hero when he sends him back to France, drawn to the loadstone rock. In the first place, he is still not acting to redress as his mother had commanded but only to plead mercy for the members and the agents of his own class. As his assumed name suggests, and it has to be significant in a novel filled with Carlyle's clothing symbols and with symbolic names, Charles Darnay is, at best, a mender, and has no place as part of a revolution. He wants reform; the Defarges, true revolutionaries, want continued abuses to infuriate the people.

In the second place, Charles's impulsive action is strongly reminiscent of the ineffective or unsustained windmill charges on social institutions made by previous romantic heroes in Dickens's novels. He dashes into the French Revolution as Arthur Clennam of *Little Dorrit* took on the Circumlocution Office or as Richard Carstone of *Bleak House* smashed his head against the Court of Chancery. The action is naively vain, as Dickens suggests when he tells us of Darnay that the "glorious vision of doing good, which is so often the sanguine mirage of so many good minds, arose before him, and he even saw himself in the illusion with some influence to guide this raging Revolution." And there is also the possibility of an unworthy subconscious motivation for his action. Since it developed from a sense of shame and guilt, Charles's purpose, like that of Clennam, may be to punish himself. Having failed to redress the wrong as his mother had charged him to do, he may be embracing the opportunity for the violent atonement she had predicted as the alternative. In any event, these are the ways Charles's brief career as a social activist seems destined to turn out—vain and self-destructive.

But before we go too far in joining the chorus which condemns Charles Darnay, it is well to remember that Dickens could never bring himself to believe in the Carlylean hero and that by this time in his career he was highly skeptical of the effectuality of social action of any sort. Dickens may not be criticizing Charles Darnay's qualities as a Revolutionary hero; he is more likely undermining the very concept of romantic heroism by doubting both its motives and its possibilities for success. Charles is at least as powerless in Revolutionary France as he was in bourgeois England, but in the long run he is no less effectual than the other would-be Revolutionary heroes whose fate Carton predicts in the final chapter.

—Edwin M. Eigner, "Charles Darnay and Revolutionary Identity," *Dickens Studies Annual* 12 (1983): 154–56

J. M. RIGNALL ON THE CONTRADICTORY NATURE OF *A TALE OF TWO CITIES*

[J. M. Rignall is a professor of English at the University of Warwick in Coventry, England. He has written *Realist*

Fiction and the Strolling Spectator (1992). In this extract, Rignall believes that there is a contradiction at the heart of *A Tale of Two Cities* between the inevitability of violence in history and a hope that violence can be ended or averted by self-sacrifice.]

It is not surprising that the most remembered scene in *A Tale of Two Cities* is the last, for this novel is dominated, even haunted, by its ending. From the opening chapter in which the "creatures of this chronicle" are set in motion "along the roads that lay before them," while the Woodman Fate and the Farmer Death go silently about their ominous work, those roads lead with sinister inevitability to the revolutionary scaffold. To an unusual extent, especially given the expansive and centrifugal nature of Dickens's imagination, this is an end-determined narrative whose individual elements are ordered by an ending which is both their goal and, in a sense, their source. In a historical novel like this there is a transparent relationship between narrative form and historical vision, and the formal features of *A Tale*—its emphatic linearity, continuity, and negative teleology—define a distinctive vision of history. As Robert Alter has argued in his fine critical account of the novel, it is not the particular historical event that ultimately concerns Dickens here, but rather a wider view of history and the historical process. That process is a peculiarly grim one. As oppression is shown to breed oppression, violence to beget violence, evil to provoke evil, a pattern emerges that is too deterministic to owe much to Carlyle and profoundly at odds with the conventional complacencies of Whig history. Instead of progress there is something more like the catastrophic continuum that is Walter Benjamin's description of the historical process: the single catastrophe, piling wreckage upon wreckage. And when, in the sentimental postscript of Carton's prophecy, Dickens finally attempts to envisage a liberation from this catastrophic process, he can only do so, like Benjamin, in eschatological terms. For Benjamin it was the messianic intervention of a proletarian revolution that would bring time to a standstill and blast open the continuum of history; for Dickens it is the Christ-like intervention of a self-sacrificing individual that is the vehicle for a vision of a better world which seems to lie beyond time and history. The parallel with Benjamin cannot be pressed beyond the common perception of a pernicious historical continuum and the common desire to break it, but the coexistence of these two elements in *A Tale* is, I wish to argue, important for an understanding of the novel, lending it a peculiarly haunted and contradictory quality as Dickens gives expression to a vision of history which both compels and repels him at the same time.

In Carton's final vision of a world seemingly beyond time, the paradigm of the apocalypse mediates between what is known of history and what may be hoped for it. That hope is not to be dismissed as mere sentimentality, whatever the manner of its expression. However inadequately realized Carton's prophecy may be in imaginative terms, it is significant as a moment of resistance to the grimly terminal linearity and historical determinism of the preceding narrative. That resistance is not confined to the last page of the novel, for, as I shall show, it manifests itself in other places and in other ways, creating a faint but discernible counter-current to the main thrust of the narrative. This is not to say that Dickens presents a thoroughgoing deconstruction of his own narrative procedures and version of history in *A Tale,* for the process at work here is more ambiguous and tentative than that. There is a struggle with sombre fears that gives rise to contradictions which cannot be reduced to the internal self-contradictions of language. What the novel presents is, rather, the spectacle of an imagination both seized by a compelling vision of history as a chain of violence, a catastrophic continuum, and impelled to resist that vision in the very act of articulation, so that the narrative seems at the same time to seek and to shun the violent finality of its ending in the Terror. The nightmare vision is too grim to accept without protest, and too powerful to be dispelled by simple hopefulness, and the work bears the signs of this unresolved and unresolvable contradiction.

—J. M. Rignall, "Dickens and the Catastrophic Continuum of History in *A Tale of Two Cities,*" *ELH* 51, No. 3 (Fall 1984): 575–76

[Ruth Glancy (b. 1948), a lecturer in English at Concordia College in Edmonton, Alberta, Canada, is the author of bibliographies of Dickens's Christmas books (1985) and of *A Tale of Two Cities* (1993) as well as a study of that novel, from which the following extract is taken. Here, Glancy focuses on the figure of Lucie Manette, finding her centrally related to all the characters in the book.]

When Dickens suggested "The Thread of Gold" for the title of the novel, he was intending it to be Lucie Manette's story. And in many ways it is. The Bastille prisoner is recalled to life through her agency; Darnay's new life is bound up with hers; Carton is inspired to his supreme sacrifice because of his love for her and his recognition of her goodness. She is central to the actions of nearly all the characters except perhaps the Crunchers: Mr. Lorry is devoted to her and acts throughout the novel largely out of this devotion; Miss Pross too is governed in her actions solely by her love of Lucie. Madame Defarge directs her anger against Lucie because she is Darnay's wife and because she therefore represents the aristocratic wife whose death will somehow compensate for the sufferings of the peasant wives and children. In many ways the characters are also paired around the central figure of Lucie. Miss Pross is pitted against Madame Defarge, and their final fatal meeting is caused by Miss Pross's attempts to prevent Madame Defarge from finding Lucie and condemning her to the tribunal. Carton and Darnay, physical doubles, are rivals for Lucie's love. Stryver and Carton both aspire to her hand, but Carton's unselfish love for her is contrasted with Stryver's selfish desire to own a wife as he would a piece of property. Darnay and Manette love her enough to share her because, as Darnay tells her, she is able to spare enough of herself to keep everyone happy.

We have seen how Lucie's characterization derived from Dickens's childhood friend Lucy Stroughill, his golden-haired neighbor, and the golden-haired Lucy from *The Wreck of the Golden Mary* who, like Lucie Manette, is the inspiration that keeps hope alive in the desperate survivors of the shipwreck.

"Lucie" means light, and both characters take on a religious significance as the possessors of a spiritual purity. The golden thread too has religious connotations. It is traditionally a metaphor for the inviolable heart of things, the sacred core of truth and honesty that binds together the more vulnerable pieces of the fabric. In English law it refers to the tenet that a man is innocent until he is proven guilty. Without the golden thread, any other virtues in the system cannot survive. And so it is with Lucie, who gives meaning and purpose to the lives of Darnay, Carton, Manette, Miss Pross, and Mr. Lorry. There are many connecting threads in the book, such as Manette's connection to Darnay and the Defarges, but whereas these threads lead to the revelation of hidden sufferings and repressed guilt, Lucie's golden thread binds the characters into an indestructible web of love that will prove stronger than Madame Defarge's powerful lust for revenge. ⟨. . .⟩

Lucie has been criticized as being a faceless character, too good to be true and lacking in dimension. Certainly her speech is often ludicrously stagy, as in her first long address to her father when the refrain "weep for it" merely adds to the sentimentality of her words. Her conversation with Carton is equally melodramatic. But we have already seen how Dickens intended the characters to be "true to nature, but whom the story should express more than they should express themselves by dialogue" (John Forster). Seen through her actions, Lucie is anything but a melodramatic stage heroine; rather, she is a courageous woman like the British women caught in the bloodbath of the Indian Massacre whom Dickens wanted to honor in *The Perils of Certain English Prisoners.* Heroic women took an increasingly major role in Dickens's later novels, perhaps through the influence of Ellen Ternan. Ellen had played the part of another heroic Lucy, Lucy Crawford in *The Frozen Deep,* and Dickens certainly was thinking of her when he named Estella in *Great Expectations* and Helena Landless in *Edwin Drood* (Ellen's middle name was Lawless). Lucie's bravery is the determined but patient courage that Dickens talked of as "quiet heroism" in *The Battle of Life.* Like Little Dorrit in the novel preceding *A Tale of Two Cities,* Lucie is the sole support of an imprisoned and sometimes mentally deranged father. Although she fears the footsteps that seem to be threatening Soho and dreads the shadow that Madame Defarge casts over her, she is resilient enough to brave the dangerous streets of Paris to stand beneath the prison wall every day, in the hopes that Darnay may see her there. The thread of gold that binds her to him would lead her, as Carton tells Mr. Lorry, to "lay her own fair head beside her husband's cheerfully" on the guillotine. Lucie's role in the book is to provide the moral center from which the people surrounding her draw their strength. She is less active than the later heroines of *Our Mutual Friend* and *Edwin Drood,* Lizzie Hexam and Helena Landless, because that sort of tough, aggressive woman is seen in Miss Pross and taken to horrifying extremes in Madame Defarge. Lizzie Hexam rescues Eugene Wrayburn (a dissolute waster like Carton) from drowning because she is a skillful oarswoman and is able to pull him to safety. Because Madame Defarge and Miss Pross share this physical strength, Lucie's strength is mental and emotional, but she exemplifies the qualities of a genuine hero: strength, dedication, patience, and bravery.

—Ruth Glancy, A Tale of Two Cities: *Dickens's Revolutionary Novel* (Boston: Twayne, 1991), pp. 94–97

TOM LLOYD ON MADAME DEFARGE

[Tom Lloyd is a professor of English at Georgia Southern University and the author of articles on Dickens and Carlyle. In this extract, Lloyd, studying the character of Madame Defarge, believes that she is a kind of force of nature parallel to the Revolution itself.]

Madame Defarge embodies in its most absolute form the inevitable release of what Schiller terms the 'crude, lawless instincts' of those repressed politically and psychologically (*Aesthetic Education* 25). Based on Mlle Théroigne in Carlyle's *The French Revolution,* she is like a force of nature whose instinctual patience is indicated by the 'register' she stores in her memory of who is to be saved and who executed once the energies of Saint Antoine are unleashed to sweep away the enervated aristocracy. Madame Defarge seems conscious of the natural energy she represents, consistently comparing the Revolution to a natural force and denying that it can be quantified or defined. For example, she tells her more conventional husband that 'it does not take a long time . . . for an earthquake to swallow a town,' but stresses the inadequacy of formulas in adding the question, 'Tell me how long it takes to prepare the earthquake?' She refuses to try to hurry the time of vengeance, saying that 'When the time comes, let loose a tiger and a devil; but wait for the time with the tiger and the devil chained.'

M. Defarge retains a need for clear definitions and manifestations of things, which his wife recognizes, telling him, 'you sometimes need to see your victim and your opportunity, to sustain you.' She regards as a weakness his desire to know when the violence will begin and end, insisting that such quantification is impossible, like trying 'to make and store the lightning.' Psychologically in a realm beyond formulas, she cannot set limits to her philosophy of 'extermination', and therefore opposes her husband's assertion that the Terror 'must stop somewhere.' But M Defarge seeks meanings even when he participates in the storming of the Bastille. Though no one is presently in the North Tower where Manette was imprisoned for eighteen years, he demands that one of the guards take him there so that he can understand the meaning of One Hundred and Five: 'Does it mean a captive, or a place of captivity? Or do you mean that I shall strike you dead?' In an environment where identities are scrambled or extinguished and people are reduced to 'ghosts' of their former selves, Defarge wants a clear definition of the mystery called Manette. The 'indifference' of the Marquis and the 'absolute' extermination of Madame Defarge are antitypes of the endeavour to connect words with things. Defarge's violent destruction of the furniture in Manette's old cell to find a written or other key to his mystery reflects a paradoxical desire to obliterate and know; we later discover that he found the manuscript in the chimney, a place of ashes as well as energy. His search is normally fruitless, for he finds only a dead text which no longer reflects the spiritual essence of its author.

In *A Tale of Two Cities* there is a non-verbal communication based on vengeance, and another based on love. Madame Defarge repudiates formulas in favour of absolute violence and mysterious signs based on knitting, roses in handkerchiefs, and noncommittal allusions to natural forces. But at a time when the word is falsified and dead, such signs are more efficacious than M Defarge's futile search for definitions amidst the carnage at the Bastille. Those able to read history—Dickens places his reader in this advantaged position—can read the non-verbal message contained in the Cross of Blood drawn in the air by Madame Defarge's brother, or the verbal sign BLOOD Gaspard scrawls on a wall with wine. But there are also transcendent non-verbal signs based on love and sympathy, for instance in the eyes of Darnay's mother, which give meaning to her assertion that he must 'have mercy and redress' the wrongs perpetrated by his family on the poor. Above all, Lucie Manette has this ability. By standing outside Darnay's Paris prison she can revitalize him, reversing his initial, precipitous slide into insanity. Madame Defarge's inability to comprehend this alternative form of communication is revealed by her plot to denounce Lucie for 'making signs and signals to prisoners.'

Yet she is forced to effect a non-verbal communication with Miss Pross in the climactic scene where the sans-culotte comes hunting for Lucie, who is in the process of escaping from Paris. Here her energies are thwarted, and she is spent like any natural storm or earthquake. The cessation of her power through Pross's pistol shot foreshadows the retreat of the violently daemonic and the reconstitution of the word, symbolized by the power of the signed papers to get Darnay (disguised as Carton), Manette, and Lucie out of the country. Like Thomas Mann's demonic Cipolla, Defarge is suddenly rendered lifeless, as though a violent disrobing of civilized control and language have played themselves out, leaving Pross deaf but free. In this grotesque encounter the two cannot understand each other's words: 'Each spoke in her own language; neither understood the other's words; both were very watchful, and intent to deduce from look and manner, what the unintelligible words meant.' Miss Pross dismisses her opponent's language as 'nonsensical.' Yet they communicate non-verbally, one motivated by the 'vigorous tenacity of love,' the other by sheer hatred. As with Darnay and his mother, and Carton and the young girl at the end of the novel, the eyes are the key to this nonrational language:

> 'It will do her no good to keep herself concealed from me at this moment,' said Madame Defarge. 'Good patriots will know what that means. Let me see her. Go tell her that I wish to see her. Do you hear?'

> 'If those eyes of yours were bed-winches,' returned Miss Pross, 'and I was an English four-poster, they shouldn't loose a splinter of me. No, you wicked foreign woman; I am your match.'

Madame Defarge's attack is a parodic version of Sydney Carton's self-sacrifice in the next chapter: 'if she had been ordered to the axe to-morrow,' her only response would have been 'a fierce desire to change places with the man who sent her there'; rendered 'lifeless' by a pistol shot, she symbolically re-enters the unseen world when Pross locks her body in and throws the key into the same river Carton has already mentally followed to death.

—Tom Lloyd, "Language, Love and Identity: *A Tale of Two Cities*," *Dickensian* 88, No. 3 (Autumn 1992): 158–60

JAMES E. MARLOW ON THE DEAD HAND OF TIME IN *A TALE OF TWO CITIES*

[James E. Marlow, a professor of English at the University of Massachusetts at Dartmouth, has written *Charles Dickens: The Uses of Time* (1994), from which the following extract is taken. Here, Marlow maintains that the central theme of *A Tale of Two Cities* is the dead hand of time weighing upon all the characters and events of the novel, but that it is counterbalanced by the theme of resurrection.]

Of all the novels by Dickens, *Little Dorrit* may illustrate the hardest and most thorough struggle over the rights and dangers of the past. Nevertheless, the struggle continues in *A Tale of Two Cities.* Albert Hutter says that "the overt and seemingly relentless subtext of this novel is to give meaning to death or to the past, to disinter the historical moment and make it come alive. The French Revolution is depicted as a natural effect of the injustices of the past; and the excesses of the revolution are a result of the carelessness and indifference broadcast by the aristocracy in the past. The warning to England was obvious: "It was much too much the way of native British orthodoxy, to talk of this terrible Revolution as if it were the one only harvest ever known under the skies that had not been sown" (2, 24). But the savagery had been sown—even as it was being sown in England, Dickens feared, in 1859.

Dickens set up the dead hand theme by treating respectable institutions with withering irony. Even venerable Tellson's Bank and its partners come in for scorn through their refusal to consider altering their old building: "In this respect the House was much on a par with the Country, which did very often disinherit its sons for suggesting improvements in laws and customs that had long been highly objectionable, but were only the more respectable" (2, 1). And the narrator grows even more incensed, reminding us of Tellson's complicity with the "putting to death [that] was a recipe so much in vogue" in the previous century. As a representative, then, of the "good old times" (garnering much of its current respectability from its antiquity), Tellson's Bank—a synecdoche for the principles of the dead hand, upon which its operation is run—is shown to be worthy of nothing but ridicule.

To the extent that the aristocrats in France depended upon the past for their privilege, to that extent did the crimes of the past have the power to destroy them. The Marquis de Evrémonde, who epitomizes the French aristocracy, sounds a reactionary note that echoes in England: "France in all such things is changed for the worse. Our not remote ancestors held the right of life and death over the surrounding vulgar" (2, 9). But the Defarges are in agreement, desiring only to maintain this ultimate right for their own use. The Defarges are the natural outgrowth of exercising such rights—the harvest of such a sowing. If Monseigneur's principles create the revolutionaries, the revolutionaries are, in their very acts of revenge, the self-appointed heirs of the very past that they are trying to extirpate. By replicating the ruthlessness of their oppressors, the victims yield to the dead hand. Their suffering has caused the sclerosis of reaction, not true change. Therefore, the dead hand does both the sowing and the reaping; and the harvest can only be death.

Resurrection is the counter-theme of *A Tale of Two Cities.* Ironically, what hope for the resurrection of humanity there is seems to be assigned to the ambivalent Jerry Cruncher and the Resurrection Men. But this is a parody of the theme, a game with the reader that Dickens could not resist playing. However, without ambivalence, Lucy is shown to be a fountain of life. Obvious and melodramatic though her function in the plot may be, the character is essential to the novel—as she and her creator are aware. "Can I not recall you" (2, 13), she says to Carton—sounding Lorry's earlier, cryptic phrase, which initiated the important motif which serves as title to Book the First, "Recalled to Life." All of France, and all of England, needed to be recalled to true life. But Carton is the prime object for resurrection because, as he says, "I am like one who died young. All my life might have been" (2, 13). Carton breaks the Dickensian mold: here is a character whose past is—nothing. It is not even suffering and humiliation. Insofar as it is "wasted forces," it is merely dead. It is as if his dialectic of the past brought Dickens again to see that suffering is not the worst legacy of the past. What is worse is a past that conveys into the present nothing to care for. In the character of Carton—often said to be in the Byronic mold of Steerforth—Dickens at last concluded that the Steerforths of the world were more unfortunate than the Copperfields. Although Edgar Johnson decried the "overindulged sentiment" in certain scenes in *A Tale of Two Cities,* the novel is an important stage in Dickens's dialectic; and it surely conveys power both in its articulation through the themes of the dead hand of the potential for renewed life, and even in the biblical resonance of Carton's last words: "I am the Resurrection and the Life, saith the Lord" (3, 15).

—James E. Marlow, *Charles Dickens: The Uses of Time* (Selinsgrove, PA: Susquehanna University Press, 1994), pp. 62–64

Books by
Charles Dickens

Sketches by "Boz," Illustrative of Every-day Life and Every-day People. 1836. 2 vols.

Sunday under Three Heads. 1836.

The Village Coquettes: A Comic Opera. 1836.

The Posthumous Papers of the Pickwick Club. 1836–37. 20 parts.

The Strange Gentleman: A Comic Burletta. 1837.

Memoirs of Joseph Grimaldi (editor). 1838. 2 vols.

Sketches of Young Gentlemen. 1838.

Oliver Twist; or, The Parish Boy's Progress. 1838. 3 vols.

The Life and Adventures of Nicholas Nickleby. 1838–39. 20 parts.

The Loving Ballad of Lord Bateman (with William Makepeace Thackeray). 1839.

Sketches of Young Couples. 1840.

Master Humphrey's Clock; The Old Curiosity Shop; Barnaby Rudge. 1840–41. 88 parts.

The Pic Nic Papers (editor). 1841. 3 vols.

American Notes. 1842. 2 vols.

A Christmas Carol in Prose: Being a Ghost-Story of Christmas. 1843.

The Life and Adventures of Martin Chuzzlewit, His Relatives, Friends and Enemies. 1843–44. 20 parts.

The Chimes: A Goblin Story of Some Bells That Rang an Old Year Out and a New Year In. 1845.

The Cricket on the Hearth: A Fairy Tale of Home. 1846.

Pictures from Italy. 1846.

The Battle of Life: A Love Story. 1846.

Dealings with the Firm of Dombey and Son Wholesale, Retail and for Exportation. 1846–48. 20 parts.

An Appeal to Fallen Women. 1847.

Works. 1847–67. 17 vols.

The Haunted Man and the Ghost's Bargain: A Fancy for Christmas Time. 1848.

Elegy Written in a Country Churchyard. c. 1849.

The Personal History, Adventures, Experiences and Observations of David Copperfield the Younger. 1849–50. 20 parts.

Mr. Nightingale's Diary: A Farce (with Mark Lemon). 1851.

Bleak House. 1852–53. 20 parts.

A Child's History of England. 1852–54. 3 vols.

Hard Times, for These Times. 1854.

Speech Delivered at the Meeting of the Administrative Reform Association. 1855.

Little Dorrit. 1855–57. 20 parts.

Novels and Tales Reprinted from Household Words (editor). 1856–59. 11 vols.

The Case of the Reformers in the Literary Fund (with others). 1858.

Speech as the Anniversary Festival of the Hospital for Sick Children. 1858.

Speech at the First Festival Dinner of the Playground and Recreation Society. 1858.

Works (Library Edition). 1858–59 (22 vols.), 1861–74 (30 vols.).

A Tale of Two Cities. 1859. 8 parts.

Christmas Stories from Household Words. 1859. 9 parts.

Great Expectations. 1861. 3 vols.

Great Expectations: A Drama. 1861.

The Uncommercial Traveller. 1861.

An Address on Behalf of the Printer's Pension Society. c. 1864.

Speech at the North London or University College Hospital: Anniversary Dinner in Aid of the Funds. 1864.

Our Mutual Friend. 1864–65. 20 parts.

The Frozen Deep (with Wilkie Collins). 1866.

No Thoroughfare (with Wilkie Collins). 1867.

Speech at the Railway Benevolent Institution: Ninth Annual Dinner. 1867.

Works (Charles Dickens Edition). 1867–75. 21 vols.

Christmas Stories from All the Year Round. c. 1868. 9 parts.

The Readings of Mr. Charles Dickens, as Condensed by Himself. 1868.

Address Delivered at the Birmingham and Midland Institute. 1869.

A Curious Dance round a Curious Tree (with W. H. Wills). 1870.

Speech as Chairman of the Anniversary Festival Dinner of the Royal Free Hospital. 1870.

The Mystery of Edwin Drood. 1870. 6 parts.

Speeches Literary and Social. Ed. R. H. Shepherd. 1870.

The Newsvendors' Benevolent and Provident Institution: Speeches in Behalf of the Institution. 1871.

Is She His Wife? or Something Singular: A Comic Burletta. c. 1872.

The Lamplighter: A Farce. 1879.

The Mudfog Papers, etc. 1880.

Letters. Ed. Georgina Hogarth and Mary Dickens. 1880–82. 3 vols.

Plays and Poems, with a Few Miscellanies in Prose Now First Collected. Ed. R. H. Shepherd. 1885. 2 vols.

The Lazy Tour of Two Idle Apprentices; No Thoroughfare; The Perils of Certain English Prisoners (with Wilkie Collins). 1890.

Works (Macmillan Edition). 1892–1925. 21 vols.

Letters to Wilkie Collins 1851–1870. Ed. Lawrence Hutton. 1892.

Works (Gadshill Edition). Ed. Andrew Lang. 1897–1908. 36 vols.

To Be Read at Dusk and Other Stories, Sketches and Essays. Ed. F. G. Kitton. 1898.

Christmas Stories from Household Words *and* All the Year Round. 1898. 5 vols.

Works (Biographical Edition). Ed. Arthur Waugh. 1902–03. 19 vols.

Poems and Verses. Ed. F. G. Kitton. 1903.

Works (National Edition). Ed. Bertram W. Matz. 1906–08. 40 vols.

Dickens and Maria Beadnell: Private Correspondence. Ed. G. P. Baker. 1908.

The Dickens-Kolle Letters. Ed. Harry B. Smith. 1910.

Works (Centenary Edition). 1910–11. 36 vols.

Dickens as Editor: Letters Written by Him to William Henry Wills, His Sub-Editor. Ed. R. C. Lehmann. 1912.

Works (Waverley Edition). 1913–18. 30 vols.

Unpublished Letters to Mark Lemon. Ed. Walter Dexter. 1927.

Letters to the Baroness Burdett-Coutts. Ed. Charles C. Osborne. 1931.

Dickens to His Oldest Friend: The Letters of a Lifetime to Thomas Beard. Ed. Walter Dexter. 1932.

Letters to Charles Lever. Ed. Flora V. Livingston. 1933.

Mr. and Mrs. Charles Dickens: His Letters to Her. Ed. Walter Dexter. 1935.

The Love Romance of Dickens, Told in His Letters to Maria Beadnell (Mrs. Winter). Ed. Walter Dexter. 1936.

The Nonesuch Dickens. Ed. Arthur Waugh, Hugh Walpole, Walter Dexter, and Thomas Hatton. 1937–38. 23 vols.

Letters. Ed. Walter Dexter. 1938. 3 vols.

The New Oxford Illustrated Dickens. 1947–58. 21 vols.

Speeches. Ed. K. J. Fielding, 1960, 1988.

Letters (Pilgrim Edition). Ed. Madeline House, Graham Storey, Kathleen Tillotson et al. 1965– .

The Clarendon Dickens. Ed. John Butt, Kathleen Tillotson, and James Kinsley. 1966– .

Uncollected Writings from Household Words *1850–1859.* Ed. Harry Stone. 1968.

Complete Plays and Selected Poems. 1970.

Dickens in Europe: Essays. Ed. Rosalind Vallance. 1975.

The Public Readings. Ed. Phillip Collins. 1975.

Supernatural Short Stories. Ed. Michael Hayes. 1978.

The Annotated Dickens. Ed. Edward Guiliano and Philip Collins. 1986. 2 vols.

Dickens' Working Notes for His Novels. Ed. Harry Stone. 1987.

Sketches by Boz and Other Early Papers 1833–39. Ed. Michael Slater. 1994.

Works about Charles Dickens and A Tale of Two Cities

Ackroyd, Peter. *Dickens.* New York: HarperCollins, 1990.

Baldridge, Cates. "Alternatives to Bourgeois Individualism in *A Tale of Two Cities.*" *Studies in English Literature 1500–1900* 30 (1990): 633–54.

Barnard, Robert. *Imagery and Theme in the Novels of Dickens.* Oslo: Universitetsforlaget, 1974.

Baumgarten, Murray. "Writing the Revolution." *Dickens Studies Annual* 12 (1983): 161–76.

Bloom, Harold, ed. *Charles Dickens.* New York: Chelsea House, 1987.

Brook, George L. *The Language of Dickens.* London: Andre Deutsch, 1970.

Butt, John, and Kathleen Tillotson. *Dickens at Work.* London: Chatto & Windus, 1958.

Carey, John. *The Violent Effigy: A Study of Dickens' Imagination.* London: Faber & Faber, 1973.

Carlisle, Janice. *The Sense of an Audience: Dickens, Thackeray, and George Eliot at Mid-Century.* Athens: University of Georgia Press, 1981.

Cockshut, A. O. J. *The Imagination of Charles Dickens.* New York: New York University Press, 1962.

Coolidge, Archibald C., Jr. *Charles Dickens as Serial Novelist.* Ames: Iowa State University Press, 1967.

Court, Franklin E. "Boots, Barbarism, and the New Order in Dickens's *Tale of Two Cities.*" *Victorians Institute Journal* 9 (1980–81): 29–37.

Daldry, Graham. *Charles Dickens and the Form of the Novel.* Totowa, NJ: Barnes & Noble, 1987.

Daleski, H. M. *Dickens and the Art of Analogy*. London: Faber & Faber, 1970.

———. "Imagining Revolution: The Eye of History and of Fiction." *Journal of Narrative Technique* 18 (1988): 61–72.

Dunn, Richard J. "A Tale of Two Dramatists." *Dickens Studies Annual* 12 (1983): 117–24.

Dyson, A. E. *The Inimitable Dickens: A Reading of the Novels*. London: Macmillan, 1970.

Fielding, K. J. *Charles Dickens: A Critical Introduction*. London: Longmans, Green, 1958.

Frank, Lawrence. *Charles Dickens and the Romantic Self*. Lincoln: University of Nebraska Press, 1984.

Giddings, Robert, ed. *The Changing World of Charles Dickens*. London: Vision Press, 1983.

Gilbert, Elliot L. " 'To Awake from History': Carlyle, Thackeray, and *A Tale of Two Cities*." *Dickens Studies Annual* 12 (1983): 247–65.

Gold, Joseph. *Charles Dickens: Radical Moralist*. Minneapolis: University of Minnesota Press, 1972.

Goldberg, Michael. *Carlyle and Dickens*. Athens: University of Georgia Press, 1972.

Guérard, Albert J. *The Triumph of the Novel: Dickens, Dostoevsky, Faulkner*. New York: Oxford University Press, 1976.

Hardy, Barbara. *The Moral Art of Dickens*. New York: Oxford University Press, 1970.

Herst, Beth F. *The Dickens Hero: Selfhood and Alienation in the Dickens World*. New York: AMS Press, 1990.

Holbrook, David. *Charles Dickens and the Image of Woman*. New York: New York University Press, 1993.

Hornback, Bert G. *"The Hero of My Life": Essays on Dickens*. Athens: Ohio University Press, 1981.

———. *"Noah's Arkitecture": A Study of Dickens's Mythology*. Athens: Ohio University Press, 1972.

Houston, Gail Turley. *Consuming Fictions; Gender, Class, and Hunger in Dickens's Novels.* Carbondale: Southern Illinois University Press, 1994.

Ingham, Patricia. *Dickens, Women, and Language.* Toronto: University of Toronto Press, 1992.

Johnson, Edgar H. *Charles Dickens: His Tragedy and Triumph.* Rev. ed. London: Allen Lane, 1977.

Kincaid, James R. *Dickens and the Rhetoric of Laughter.* Oxford: Clarendon Press, 1971.

Kucich, John. *Excess and Restraint in the Novels of Charles Dickens.* Athens: University of Georgia Press, 1981.

Leavis, F. R., and Q. D. Leavis. *Dickens the Novelist.* London: Chatto & Windus, 1970.

Lettis, Richard. *The Dickens Aesthetic.* New York: AMS Press, 1989.

Lindley, Dwight N. "Clio and Three Historical Novels." *Dickens Studies Annual* 10 (1982): 77–99.

Lucas, John. *The Melancholy Man: A Study of Dickens's Novels.* Totowa, NJ: Barnes & Noble, 1980.

Manheim, Leonard. "A Tale of Two Characters: A Study in Multiple Projection." *Dickens Studies Annual* 1 (1970): 225–37.

Manning, Sylvia Bank. *Dickens as Satirist.* New Haven: Yale University Press, 1971.

Miller, J. Hillis. *Charles Dickens: The World of His Novels.* Cambridge, MA: Harvard University Press, 1958.

Miyoshi, Masao. *The Divided Self: A Perspective on the Literature of the Victorians.* New York: New York University Press, 1969.

Monod, Sylvère. *Dickens the Novelist.* Norman: University of Oklahoma Press, 1968.

Morgan, Nicholas H. *Secret Journeys: Theory and Practice in Reading Dickens.* Rutherford, NJ: Fairleigh Dickinson University Press, 1992.

Nelson, Harland S. *Charles Dickens.* Boston: Twayne, 1981.

———. "Shadow and Substance in *A Tale of Two Cities.*"
Dickensian 84 (1988): 97–106.

Newcomb, Mildred. *The Imagined World of Charles Dickens.*
Columbus: Ohio State University Press, 1989.

Nisbet, Ada, and Blake Nevius, ed. *Dickens Centennial Essays.*
Berkeley: University of California Press, 1971.

Page, Norman. *A Dickens Companion.* London: Macmillan,
1984.

Pratt, Branwen Bailey. "Carlyle and Dickens: Heroes and Hero-
Worshipers." *Dickens Studies Annual* 12 (1983): 223–46.

Praz, Mario. "Charles Dickens." In Praz's *The Hero in Eclipse in
Victorian Fiction.* Tr. Angus Davidson. London: Oxford
University Press, 1956, pp. 127–88.

Raina, Badri. *Dickens and the Dialectic of Growth.* Madison:
University of Wisconsin Press, 1986.

Robson, Lisa. "The 'Angels' in Dickens's House: Representation
of Women in *A Tale of Two Cities.*" *Dalhousie Review* 72
(1992): 311–33.

Sanders, Andrew. *A Companion to* A Tale of Two Cities.
London: Unwin Hyman, 1988.

Schad, John. *The Reader in the Dickensian Mirror: Some New
Language.* New York: St. Martin's Press, 1992.

Schwarzbach, F. W. *Dickens and the City.* London: Athlone
Press, 1979.

Slater, Michael, ed. *Dickens 1970: Centenary Essays.* London:
Chapman & Hall, 1970.

Solomon, Pearl Chesler. *Dickens and Melville in Their Time.*
New York: Columbia University Press, 1975.

Spence, Gordon. "Dickens as a Historical Novelist." *Dickensian*
72 (1976): 21–30.

Stewart, Garrett. *Dickens and the Trials of Imagination.*
Cambridge, MA: Harvard University Press, 1974.

Stoehr, Taylor. *Dickens: The Dreamer's Stance.* Ithaca, NY: Cornell University Press, 1965.

Stone, Harry. *Dickens and the Invisible World: Fairy Tales, Fantasy, and Novel-Making.* Bloomington: Indiana University Press, 1979.

―――. *The Night Side of Dickens: Cannibalism, Passion, Necessity.* Columbus: Ohio State University Press, 1994.

Sucksmith, Harvey Peter. *The Narrative Art of Charles Dickens.* Oxford: Clarendon Press, 1970.

Thurley, Geoffrey. *The Dickens Myth: Its Genesis and Structure.* London: Routledge & Kegan Paul, 1976.

Timko, Michael. "Splendid Impressions and Picturesque Means: Dickens, Carlyle, and the French Revolution." *Dickens Studies Annual* 12 (1983): 177–95.

Vogel, Jane. *Allegory in Dickens.* University: University of Alabama Press, 1977.

Welsh, Alexander. *The City of Dickens.* Oxford: Clarendon Press, 1971.

―――. *From Copyright to Copperfield: The Identity of Dickens.* Cambridge, MA: Harvard University Press, 1987.

Williams, Raymond. *The English Novel: From Dickens to Lawrence.* London: Chatto & Windus, 1970.

Index of
Themes and Ideas